Canadian Broadcast News The Basics

Canadian Broadcast News The Basics

Brian Green
NIAGARA COLLEGE

NELSON

THOMSON LEARNING

Australia • Canada • Mexico • Singapore • Spain • United Kingdom • United States

ISBN-13: 978-0-7747-3733-3
ISBN-10: 0-7747-3733-6

For more information contact
Nelson Thomson Learning,
1120 Birchmount Road,
Scarborough, Ontario, M1K 5G4.
Or you can visit our Internet site at http://www.nelson.com

Canadian Cataloguing in Publication Data

Green, Brian
  Canadian broadcast news: the basics

Previously published under title: Broadcast news essentials.
Includes index.
ISBN 0-7747-3733-6

1. Broadcast journalism – Canada. I. Title. II. Title: Broadcast news essentials.

PN4784.B75G74 2001   070.1'9'0971   C00-931960-3

Acquisitions Editor: Anne Williams
Developmental Editor: Camille Isaacs
Production Editor: Linh Vu/Laurie Thomas
Production Co-ordinator: Cheri Westra

Copy Editor: Dallas Harrison
Cover and Interior Design: Sonya V. Thursby, Opus House Incorporated
Typesetting and Assembly: Brian Lehen • Graphic Design Ltd.
Printing and Binding: Transcontinental Printing Inc.

Cover art: Copyright © Andrew Judd, Masterfile

This book was printed in Canada.
6 7 TC 09 08

Preface

Canadian radio and television news is different from American news. It is also different from British news, although a superficial and easy description is that it lies somewhere between the two. Historically, our journalistic tradition owes more to Britain than to the United States in both print and broadcast; today, our journalism is naturally closer to the American style. The Canadian Broadcasting Corporation, probably the most influential organization in the development of Canadian broadcasting, was supposed to be a copy of the British Broadcasting Corporation. Luckily, it didn't turn out that way. Our unique compromise of public and private broadcasters working side by side — competing, co-operating, criticizing, exchanging ideas and personnel — has become the model for many countries around the world whose earlier experiments with wholly state-run or entirely free-enterprise broadcast systems weren't satisfactory.

Our news is much more issue oriented than American news, emphasizing background, context, and meaning instead of events alone. Canadians have always had a taste for serious news as provided by the documentaries of the National Film Board, the in-depth coverage of *W5* (the longest running of all news magazine shows) and *The Fifth Estate*, and the information programming of CBC Radio: *As It Happens*, *Sunday Morning*, *The House*, and so on. Even our longest-running TV game show, *Front Page Challenge*, was centred on the news.

The differences between our countries geographically, socially, and politically also help to account for the variations in news coverage. Compared with the United States, Canada simply doesn't have as many murders, fires, drug busts, police shootouts, hurricanes, earthquakes, gangs, riots, elections, trials, or robberies. The differences in content of the news and depth of the coverage have produced differences in style. While it would be difficult to describe an individual story or even a single newscast as "stylistically Canadian," overall in Canada, unlike south of the border (with notable exceptions on the Public Broadcasting Service), the style owes more to informing and less to entertaining.

This text attempts to reflect and encourage Canadian characteristics in the style of writing suggested, in the examples of news coverage given, and in all contextual and stylistic elements. My hope is that young broadcasters will continue to develop a uniquely Canadian style in the dissemination of news.

To the Instructor

This book is designed to provide basic information about writing and reporting the news in a Canadian context. While the college-level student in a journalism or broadcast program is the book's primary focus, the professional broadcaster might find the text useful as a reference and refresher. The instruction units deal with the essentials of collecting, writing, preparing, and delivering the news in both radio and television environments and are reinforced with many practical exercises and assignments. The unit on "Journalism and Society" helps to put the craft of news gathering, writing, and broadcasting in a broader frame, encouraging reflection on what we do as journalists and how we do it.

The layout of this book puts all the skills and considerations common to both radio and television first: determining what is newsworthy; news writing and reporting; basic delivery; and ethical, legal, and philosophical reflections. It then has units that apply these principles specifically, first to radio and then to television. Since every instructor approaches the teaching and learning of such diverse skills differently, the units have been designed to be largely self-contained. They may be read in virtually any order. Learners who are not interested in television, for example, will miss nothing they need to become skilful radio journalists by skipping Part 3. Teachers who prefer that their students begin writing news before moving on to news gathering and news values may reverse Units One and Two without compromising the effectiveness of the instruction or exercises.

Canadian Broadcast News includes many changes suggested by teachers who have used the book since it was first published as *Broadcast News Essentials* in 1996. The order in which some units appear has been changed to reflect more common practice among instructors; little-used sections have been deleted; requests for further detail and a more "patient" approach to difficult concepts such as "writing for the ear" and "the lead" have been addressed; and a much enhanced and updated section on television reporting, including a thorough look at videography, has been included. Want ads for broadcast journalists have been interspersed throughout later chapters to give students an indication of the skills required in the work world. Overall, the book has been strengthened, streamlined, and polished from the first edition. It does retain its student-centred approach, with friendly and clear instruction, many practical exercises to reinforce learning, and answers to selected exercises to encourage self-study.

To the Student

Many professions are taught from textbooks, and many are learned on the job, but few afford beginners an opportunity to study intensely and in detail the top practitioners at work. Broadcasting is by definition a public business, and anyone wanting to learn that business can study, critique, emulate, and second-guess the professionals anytime. Anyone interested in becoming a broadcaster who doesn't do so is wasting the best resource available. Students wanting to break into the field and professionals at every level should constantly monitor the newscasts of each local station on the dial as well as the networks and the Americans. Listening to and watching the news (and reading every available newspaper) should be a regular part of the day's activities, not just to hear and see the style of delivery and the quality of writing, editing, and production, but also to learn about and understand the events that are the raw material of every newscast.

Journalism students must be familiar with current events, and they must have a basic understanding of the issues that dominate the news — the backgrounds, the reasons, the politics behind what is reported. Courses of study and wide reading in modern history, politics, and geography are immensely helpful in writing and delivering stories that are accurate, complete, and authoritative. Journalists are required to sound knowledgeable about such a wide range of subjects and issues that anyone who is not widely read, always open to new learning opportunities, and constantly curious should probably re-examine her or his vocation.

And, of course, clear, correct, and stylish writing is a requirement. No broadcast journalism text can hope to teach writing. They all teach adaptation: adapting already competent writing to the special requirements of radio and television news.

If you are a good writer, curious about everything, and interested in current events, history, civics, communication, sociology, and politics, you will love being a journalist . . . and, with dedication and practice, you will become very good at it.

Acknowledgements

A special acknowledgement must be made of the contribution of Bill Boehlen, professor of media and television at Niagara College, who is largely responsible for the new section on videography. Bill was the first teacher in Canada to develop a separate college course specifically to train videographers, and his expertise and teaching ability are reflected in this important chapter.

Thanks to Ron Tufts, Greg Darling, Tom Pagonis, Alysha Henderson, Stu Black, Chris Jeanneret, and Eric Sorensen for expert input and assistance.

Thanks also to the market research participants who helped to shape the revisions to this book: Michael Thurnell, Conestoga College; John Rafferty, Confederation College; Susan Belyea, New Brunswick Community College; Len Arminio, Loyalist College; Veryl Todd, Lethbridge Community College; Rob Dykstra, Langara College; Jane Harrison, Loyalist College; Wayne Macdonald, New Brunswick Community College; and Mike McVeigh, Canadore College.

The experiences, learning results, and feedback of hundreds of first-year broadcast journalism students over the past decade have been vital in shaping this book to assist those students to come.

And thanks to Niagara College for the sabbatical years that made the writing and revision of this book possible.

A NOTE FROM THE PUBLISHER

Thank you for selecting *Canadian Broadcast News: The Basics*, by Brian Green. The editor and publisher have devoted considerable time to the careful development of this book. We appreciate your recognition of this effort and accomplishment.

We want to hear what you think about *Canadian Broadcast News*. Please take a few minutes to fill in the stamped reader reply card at the end of the book. Your comments and suggestions will be valuable to us as we prepare new editions and other books.

Contents

PART 1

Broadcast Journalism

UNIT 1

Broadcast News

1

What Is News?

News is the significant, the unusual, that which affects us. There have been many attempts to formulate what news is so that journalists can have a handy guideline to evaluate the events with which they deal. One formula says that news is whatever affects us in the "head, heart, and pocketbook." Another, which pulls five factors together into what the authors call the "5 Ps" of electronic news judgement, was put forward in Ross and Doreen Boynton's book *Sweepers in the Corridors of Power*: perishability, proximity, prominence, peculiarity, and probable effect.

Of course, any such formula is useful only to develop good news instincts. Most newspeople never consciously think through *why* something is news or which news event is more important than another — they just *know*. This doesn't mean that every newsperson is going to agree on the relative importance of stories or even on which stories should make a newscast and which should be cut. Each individual develops a unique news sense based on that person's values and experience and character — and on some universally agreed notions of what news is. It is these "universally agreed notions" that news judgement formulas try to address. What follows is a list of seven news values that are generally agreed to be important. They are used in two ways:

- to assist in arranging the facts in a story by helping you to determine which facts are most important and which have lesser value as news
- to assist in arranging the order of the stories in a newscast by indicating which are more "newsworthy" and therefore more important.

Proximity

This means "closeness." The nearer a story is to your broadcast audience, the more news value it has. A car accident in which three people are killed in Tucson is unlikely to make it into your newscast, but a similar incident in your town will probably be an important news item. Your audience will want to know who was killed, where it happened, and how it happened. Such a tragedy might affect them directly or indirectly in many ways.

Immediacy

"If it ain't *new*, it ain't *news*." The more recent an event, the more value it has in a newscast. A minor traffic mishap in which no one was injured but traffic on a main street was temporarily delayed will have no significance two hours after it happened, but while traffic is backed up, it might well lead a newscast. Newspapers and magazines have several advantages over the electronic media, but one great advantage of radio and TV is *immediacy*. If the electronic media are not immediate, then they give away their biggest edge to the competition.

Human Interest

This almost indefinable term often comes down to the "heart." Any story involving animals or children or old people usually has an element of human interest. Anything humorous, wildly improbable, or beyond the ordinary experience of most people would also qualify. "Dog Bites Man" is not news. "Man Bites Dog" — that's news! The re-uniting of siblings separated at infancy has no other news value except the "heartwarming" quality of human interest. The same is true of the cat that was lost for three years and returned home one day, the thief who returned his loot in a fit of remorse, the 80-year-old man who ran a marathon, and so on. Most (not all) human interest stories are placed last in a newscast to separate them from the normally serious news of the day and to give the newscast an upbeat ending.

Impact

Events that will affect your listeners have significant news value, whether the effect is on their health, wealth, environment, social relationships, or emotions. The closing of a local plant has both proximity and impact. The discovery of a cure for baldness has impact. The decline of real estate values, the rise in the cost of living, an unexpected tax reduction for homeowners: they all have impact on those who tune in to your station. Impact stories are sometimes not local or immediate, and often they require an alert newsperson to spot them. A devastating fire at a plant in Japan might pass unnoticed by the Canadian media until it is discovered that the plant supplied about 60 percent of the world's computer memory chips. The price of memory-enhancement chips for home and business computers takes a significant jump around the world as a result of the fire — impact.

Prominence of the People Involved

What happens to a famous person, one whose name is known to your entire audience, is news. The divorce of two famous movie stars is news. That Greg Perkins and his wife of seven years, Gina, who live at 789 Oak Street in your town, are splitting up is probably not news.

Sex

Yes, anything involving sex has more news value than stories that have no sex angle. A politician caught driving drunk or submitting false expense claims is serious enough, but the same politician being found on a prostitute's list of clients or frequenting a notorious massage parlour will be ensured major news coverage. Most often sex is an added factor in a story that is already newsworthy for one of the other reasons, but an element of sex in any story will, for good or ill, add weight to the story.

Production

Any story that has good pictures or sound is much more valuable than one that does not. There is a famous instance in which the CBC national news spent the whole day getting its lead story about the Crowsnest freight rates ready. Just before air time, aerial photos of a plane crash in Tokyo arrived over the satellite feed. The video footage was so compelling that the important Canadian story was pushed into second place, and the CBC led the newscast with the sensational shots of the crippled and burning airplane. An interview with a participant in an event, sounds of a crowd chanting, pictures of a location — any video or audio enhancement adds news value to any story, bumping it up in the newscast lineup.

Most stories will have a combination of these factors as well as several less tangible news values such as suspense or conflict. In judging the value of a story, you will have to determine the number of these factors present and assess the extent to which each factor is important. Even with such a list of factors, there is a great deal of subjective judging in the process of ranking facts. Practice will make you much better at it, and so will listening to and watching many professional newscasts. Eventually, your news instinct, based on a set of values like this one, will take over, and you'll *know* which stories will lead your newscast without really worrying about it. Until then, refer to these news values to determine the relative importance of the material. Remember, too, that everyone has a slightly different set of news values, and you may have to adapt your judgement to fit in with the values of your editor, news director, or even station policy.

Exercise 1.1

Put a check mark next to the story that has the greater news value in the following pairs. Referring to the news values above, indicate *why* you chose the story that you did. There are no answers given for this exercise, so it can form the basis for a discussion of news values.

1. ❏ Sarah Jackfish and her husband, Dan White, came to town yesterday to visit their son, Dr. Terry White, for the holidays.
   ❏ Baseball legend Sam Torrence stopped in town for an hour yesterday to say hello to his sister, Stella Torrence, a real estate broker.

2. ❏ Residents spoke out against Erika's Emporium of Exotic Entertainment, a strip bar proposed for a mostly residential neighbourhood, at last night's city council meeting.
   ❏ Residents spoke out against a rezoning application that would permit high-rise development in a part of town previously restricted to single-family dwellings at last night's city council meeting.

3. ❏ The condition of a local man remains critical this morning. He was the driver of a car that went out of control and hit a hydro pole late last night.
   ❏ Police are at the scene of an accident at a major intersection. Two people have been slightly injured.

4. ❏ Scientists report that they have discovered a chemical that, with a single treatment, prevents tooth decay for a lifetime.
   ❏ Astronomers say that they have discovered what they think is another planet in the solar system.

5. ❏ A man who was buried by an avalanche in Switzerland three days ago has been found alive.

❏ A three-year-old girl who disappeared from her stroller while her mother was shopping, has been found safe in a nearby toy store after a 12-hour search.

6. ❏ A major winter storm is moving this way and will hit this region during the night, depositing up to 12 centimetres of snow.
   ❏ More than 100 people are feared dead in a typhoon that swept across two provinces of India yesterday.

7. ❏ The family of a prominent businessman is going to court to contest his will, which leaves half his fortune to the public library.
   ❏ The family of a prominent businessman is going to court to contest his will, which leaves half his fortune to a young prostitute.

8. ❏ A local high school student has won a major role in a Hollywood film.
   ❏ A well-known actress has been nominated for her third Academy Award.

9. ❏ A sergeant with the city police force has been given a medal for community service.
   ❏ A sergeant with the city police force has been arrested for a series of break and enters.

10. ❏ Duties dropped as a result of the GATT Treaty will mean a reduction in egg prices of about ten cents a dozen at supermarkets beginning on Tuesday.
    ❏ Duties dropped as a result of the GATT Treaty will mean a reduction in pipe-fitting machinery of about ten percent over the next two years.

11. ❏ The new heavyweight boxing champion was crowned last night in Las Vegas.
    ❏ The new welterweight boxing champion was crowned last night in Las Vegas.

12. ❏ A popular local teacher has died of AIDS-related causes.
    ❏ The six-year-old daughter of a popular local teacher has died of AIDS-related causes.

13. ❏ Police exchanged shots with a robbery suspect in a crowded mall this morning.
    ❏ This morning, police arrested and charged three people in connection with the murder of a convenience store owner last month.

14. ❏ Firefighters from three jurisdictions are trying to put out a fire in an abandoned warehouse.

❑ Investigators from the fire marshall's office are trying to determine whether arson was the cause of the fire that killed a local resident yesterday.

15. ❑ Member of Parliament Diana Horvath was asked to leave the House of Commons yesterday for wearing shorts and a see-through blouse.

❑ Councillor Diana Horvath was charged yesterday with accepting a bribe from a developer.

Newscast Lineup

The lineup is the order in which the stories will appear during the newscast. Four factors influence the placement of stories: news judgement, grouping of similar stories, station policy, and availability of inserts.

NEWS JUDGEMENT

Ideally, perhaps, your professional judgement of the value of the stories to your audience should be the only factor dictating where stories go in a newscast. And, indeed, it is the most important factor. The story with the most "points" on your scale of news values becomes the first story in the newscast. Subsequent stories are arranged in descending order of importance, down to the story that has the least news value in your judgement. This is a good way to start assembling the newscast; then use the other factors to modify this "ideal" order.

GROUPING OF SIMILAR STORIES

To make the newscast flow, to give it a sense of unity, it is a good idea to link stories that have something in common. This may mean pulling a story out of its placement in the lineup and bumping it up or down to get it next to a compatible story. For example, a couple of stories about labour disputes or settlements make a natural group. Two or three government or political stories might be placed together. By grouping stories, you give the newscast a pattern rather than jar your audience with leaps from Parliament to a strike, then back to Parliament, then on to a labour settlement, then who knows where? Such linking can be emphasized with transitional words between the stories without suggesting that they are the same story. "While the civil servants are angry about slow progress on their contract, there's news of a settlement in another labour disagreement. . . ." "Later on

Parliament Hill, politicians turned their attention to another controversial issue. . . ."

STATION POLICY

Some stations have news policies that must be observed regardless of the merits of individual stories. For example, there might be a standard policy that the six o'clock newscast begin with a local story no matter what is going on outside the local viewing or listening area. Other non-editorial factors in the lineup may include a requirement that a light or upbeat story appear just before or just after a commercial break. Your judgement of how a newscast should line up may have to be adapted to such requirements.

AVAILABILITY OF INSERTS

Stories with video- or audiotape inserts should, whenever possible, be spaced throughout the newscast. While this guideline ought to be secondary to the other considerations, it is important. Using all the stories with inserts in the first half of a newscast means that the second half will simply be story after story read by the anchor — boring for listeners or viewers and tiring for the anchor.

We will return to assembling a newscast in Chapter 23 when discussing television specifically; however, much of the information there can also be applied to radio. For now, think carefully about the relative news values of stories and analyze the newscast lineups that you hear and see.

Exercise 1.2

Number the following stories to indicate their order in a newscast for a station in your immediate locality — maybe even the college radio station. Remember to use your news judgement and to group like stories where appropriate. Suggested answers begin on page 223.

1. _____ fire in a local restaurant . . . one firefighter injured
   _____ fisheries minister announces further cutbacks to fishing on east coast
   _____ mayor announces his intention to run again in municipal elections
   _____ violence in South Africa kills four
   _____ firefighters' wage dispute with city government settled without strike

_____ premier appoints a commission to study violence in sports

_____ picket violence reported at city hospital where support staff are on strike

2. _____ land claim settlement reached with northern Saskatchewan Natives

_____ Canadian peacekeepers leaving for duty in Middle East

_____ earthquake shakes northern Japan . . . no injuries reported

_____ car accident on highway kills two local teens, four hurt

_____ gas leak closes city high school, everyone evacuated

_____ minister of defence announces purchase of new tanks for army

_____ hurricane threatens coast of Florida, could be worst in years

_____ famous movie actor arrested for possession of drugs

3. _____ United Nations begins hearings on the destruction of the rain forest in South America

_____ Ford of Canada announces sales increase of 15 percent over last year

_____ two teenagers arrested for vandalism in city cemetery

_____ China and Taiwan begin talks leading to economic co-operation

_____ protesters in British Columbia block logging trucks to prevent clearcutting

_____ city council announces layoffs of city workers but no tax increases

_____ local college student wins national broadcast journalism award

Assignments

1. Arrange to record two newscasts on different stations at the same time. List the stories and note where they are in a different order or where entirely different stories have been used. Account for the differences between the stations.
2. Clip ten or 15 stories from a newspaper and discuss with a small group the appropriate order for these stories in a radio newscast.
3. Record a TV newscast and note how many of the stories have taped inserts. With a stopwatch, time how long the anchor is actually on the screen during the newscast. Are there more stories with tape near the beginning or the end of the newscast? Why? Account for the order of the stories in this newscast lineup.

2

Where Does News Come From?

News comes from many different sources. The bulk of material that eventually goes to air, however, comes to the station "secondhand" — that is, it hasn't been directly observed by the station's reporters. Most of this secondhand material comes into the newsroom on the newswire and via satellite audio and video feeds and is provided by a news collection agency. Other sources of secondhand news include newspapers, news releases, and prepared statements. Even when a reporter provides the news, chances are that the information is still secondhand, from a phone call to a police station or fire department or from an interview with someone who was at the event. Reporters and newswriters must take the information from these sources, organize and make sense of it, confirm its validity and accuracy, and put it into a useful format for their audiences.

News Services

These services are often called "newswires," a term from the days when the newsroom had a noisy teletype machine fed by a land wire provided by the telephone or telegraph company. Now, of course, satellites feed the information directly into the newsroom's computers and/or printers. Despite the change in technology, the principle remains the same: a large organization collects information from its reporters, correspondents, and sources around the world, collates and organizes it, and sends it, more or less packaged, to newsrooms that pay the organization very well for this service. Because most radio and television stations do not have the resources to keep reporters in London and Moscow, Jerusalem and Paris, Washington and Cape Town (let alone Ottawa, Toronto, Montreal, Halifax, and Vancouver), they must subscribe to the services provided by a news-gathering organization.

The best known of these organizations are Reuters, Associated Press (AP), and United Press International (UPI). In Canada, we have Canadian Press (CP) to provide domestic information and information about international events of interest to Canadians. Several news-gathering organizations tailor their services to broadcast media. Broadcast News (BN), a division of CP, provides wire service in broadcast style, even packaged into newscasts of five minutes or three minutes, with all sorts of other information such as weather, sports, background news, stock reports, agricultural reports, and much more.

This service also provides voice feeds to radio stations for an additional fee. A recording device (recorder or disk storage) at the station is automatically activated by a signal from the satellite, and voice reports, interviews, wild sounds, and actualities (voices of the participants in an event) can then be used by the newsroom. In modern newsrooms, the voice material is stored in a computer, where it can be electronically edited using software such as SAW (Software Audio Workshop) or other dedicated audio-editing packages.

Such "audio work stations" capture audio, display it graphically as sound waves, play it back, allow it to be edited, re-edited, and manipulated — all from a computer screen. Then, when it's time for the edited clip to be played on air during a newscast, it is available at the touch of a key on the computer keyboard. Newsrooms are converting to desktop editing and playback, abandoning tapes, cassettes, and editing blocks.

Other organizations provide video feeds in much the same way so that TV newsrooms have access to pictures of events from around the world, sometimes with reporters on camera, sometimes with just raw footage of the event. The three major American networks sell these services, as do Cable News Network, Visnews (a branch of Reuters), and several smaller independent video news-gathering organizations.

Newspapers

Although broadcast newspeople don't often like to admit it, one important source of information, especially at the local level, is the newspapers. The papers also subscribe to wire services for their international and national news, but each paper has a staff of reporters to report events in the community that the paper serves. Because broadcast newsrooms (especially at most small radio stations) do not have the luxury of a stable of reporters, they often rely on the newspapers for their local information. Even large newsrooms subscribe to several papers for in-depth, background, and broad coverage, because it is a professional duty of every newsperson to be as well informed as possible.

It is both unethical and illegal for broadcast outlets to present news taken wholly from the newspapers without acknowledging the sources. Most newspapers have copyright protection for their stories, but few would object to their stories being broadcast if they receive credit. A common practice in broadcast newsrooms is to use a newspaper story as a beginning point and then to research, develop, and update the story, adding audio or video inserts if possible. A desk reporter at a radio station might read in the morning newspaper about a local resident who just won a national competition for computer art. The reporter would phone the winner and record a short interview and then, using the newspaper report for background and a couple of clips from the interview, construct two or three stories for the day's newscasts. She might even follow up with a call to the contest organizers, the winner's art teacher, or the computer magazine in which the winning entries are to be printed.

Of course, most stations monitor each other's broadcasts to check if someone else has a story that they missed. Television, with its less frequent newscasts, can take advantage of radio's hourly newscasts to check for breaking stories.

Phone-Outs

Regular checks with the police and fire departments are a routine part of newsroom activity for every shift. Normally, the same contact person (often the dispatcher) is used whenever a call is made, and it is part of that person's job to provide news outlets with whatever information is authorized for release. Larger stations have reporters who cover only police matters (see "Reporters" below), but most smaller stations rely on phone checks to get whatever information they can. (For specific information on techniques and suggestions for phone-outs, see Chapter 9.)

One of the newsroom's most valuable items is its Rolodex or phone list. It should contain the names of people to contact for every sort of story — all the local politicians, union leaders, heads of service clubs, spokespeople for every large employer in town, and local experts who can comment on everything from the economy to the Olympics. A particularly fruitful source of expertise in some communities is the college or university; many professors are published experts in their fields and are usually willing to have their observations quoted. These sources should not be overused, but they can add depth, local input, and audio or video inserts to your coverage of an issue. Whenever you make a valuable contact or get a useful quotation, make sure that the person's name is on the station's phone list for future reference.

Reporters

Most reporters respond to events that the station hears about through one of the sources mentioned. A news director or assignment editor will send a reporter to cover an event that has significant enough potential to justify the use of expensive personnel. At larger stations, a reporter will be assigned a beat and is then responsible for covering everything that goes on in that area. Typically, reporters will be assigned beats that cover police and fire, entertainment, city government, sports, business, or labour.

The advantages of beat assignments are many. Reporters can become experts in their assigned areas and thus ask the relevant questions and take shortcuts to the important issues. They can develop personal contacts with the significant people in the area, getting access when necessary.

General reporters, on the other hand, must have or acquire expertise on any number of wide-ranging issues that might come up during the day. Often the same reporter will cover every meeting of city council so that he or she can get to know the issues, the politicians, and the civil servants. However, that reporter may cover a trial the next day, a garden show and a major fire the next, and so on.

News Releases and News Conferences

Many organizations, government agencies, and special-interest groups send news of their events or activities to broadcast newsrooms. While they are most often single-page announcements, sometimes they are impressively packaged, with video- or audiotape and glossy paper with charts and illustrations included. News conferences are organized so that someone can make a statement to all the media at once instead of to each interested radio station, newspaper, and TV station. Such conferences are controlled events, with the speaker's point of view usually presented without interruption, rebuttal, or questions (at least until the end and only for as long as the speaker is comfortable). Covering such staged events is much like writing a story from a news release: it requires care to make sure the story is news that your audience wants or needs to hear, not merely a free commercial or announcement for whoever arranged the conference or sent the release. A healthy dose of scepticism should accompany any reporter who covers a media conference or receives a news release. Both should be treated as a beginning point for a story, not accepted as the full story, no matter how professionally presented and packaged they are.

Assignment

Monitor a complete television or radio newscast, and for each story try to determine the station's source for the information. Sometimes a source will be given, but in other cases you will have to speculate. A "source" column would be a useful addition to your ongoing listening log (Unit 1 Review Assignment).

"Telling" the News

Writing for the Ear

All the writing you have done up to now has been for the eye: that is, a reader scans your writing and absorbs the meaning silently. Essays, reports, letters, e-mail, all the English assignments you did in school, shopping lists — they're all meant to be read silently. Now you are being asked to write for the ear; your words will be heard, not seen. There is a huge difference in writing for the ear instead of for the eye, and you must adjust your writing in some significant ways to become good at it.

What happens when you write for a listener instead of a reader? For one thing, a listener hears your words *only once*, and then they are gone forever. A reader, on the other hand, can stop and reread, read more slowly, skip back to check a fact, stop and think about what you've said and then pick up again, or skim over material that isn't interesting. This means that, when writing for a listener, your writing must be clear, concise, and easy to understand, in both content and style. On one hearing, a listener should be able to understand and retain what information you have conveyed. The first law of broadcast newswriting, then, is KISS: keep it short and simple!

Print versus Broadcast Writing

Read an article in a newspaper. You'll notice that the story is told with all the details, all the facts, figures, and statistics, all the names, titles, and organizations, all the information that the reporter has been able to obtain — it's all there. Newspaper readers have the time to slow down, go back over details, and reread the piece if they're interested enough. Or they can simply read the first few lines of the story and skip the rest if they don't want or need any more detail. Unfortunately, a listener can't do any of those things. The result is that, as newswriters, we must tailor our stories for listeners by omitting numbers and names, cutting back on details, and making our information interesting and easy to understand *on one hearing*.

Here's an example. The first passage is from a newspaper article. The second is as this story might appear in broadcast copy. Notice the differences.

RIO DE JANEIRO — Soaring inflation, low salaries, and high unemployment in the past three years have reduced Brazilians' sex drive, a poll published in this week's *Istoe* magazine shows. In a survey by *Istoe* and the Bras-market polling firm, 67.4 percent of those interviewed said the economic crisis yielded impotence, frigidity, and a lack of sexual desire. The national average for sexual relations in this period fell from three times a week to 1.6. "You cannot be a victim on the streets and a hero in bed," psycho-therapist Moacir Costa was quoted by the magazine as saying. The poll has a margin of error of less than three percentage points.

Source: Adapted from Reuters News Agency.

Brazil's weak economy isn't very sexy. According to a poll published this week, the economy is to blame for reduced sex drive, impotence, and frigidity among a majority of Brazilians. The poll found that, over the past three years, the national average for sexual relations fell from three times a week to just over one and a half times.

Examining these two versions, you should notice several major differences. Did you spot the difference in the lengths of the sentences? the rounding off of some numbers and the leaving out of others? the omission of names, quotations, and most details? Did you get a sense that the broadcast copy is more relaxed, conversational, more the way you might tell the story verbally? On the other hand, if you want details, names, figures, and precise information, then print is the place to get them.

Another difference between a listener and a reader has to do with the expectations each has about the material you are writing. A reader expects the writing to be somewhat formal, the sentences fully punctuated, and the vocabulary rather sophisticated. A listener is used to conversation, which isn't as carefully planned as writing: sentences are not formally constructed; punctuation is provided by tone of voice, pauses, and emphasis; and vocabulary is colloquial and very simple. While a newscaster should never, even in the most informal news delivery, stoop to the stumbling, repetitious, sloppy style of true conversation, broadcast style can be informal and colloquial compared with print style. For example, contractions such as "you're" or "there's" or "it's" are encouraged in broadcast style, whereas in print these contractions would be spelled "you are," "there is," or "it is" in most kinds of writing.

Many of the formats and conventions of broadcast style that we will examine in the next chapter are designed to make writers better at writing for the ear. For now, though, we can follow several guidelines in changing our writing from "eye-oriented" to "ear-oriented."

Tip 1. *Sentences should be short and simple.* Any sentence in broadcast copy that is three lines or more of standard typing should be carefully examined to see if it can be revised and shortened.

Tip 2. *Factual details, numbers, statistics, names, and titles should be kept to a minimum.* If the name of a person or organization is not necessary to understand the story, use only the person's position or title or the organization's function (as in the example above). Include only as much detail as is necessary for a basic understanding; more is confusing and won't be remembered anyway.

Tip 3. *Language should be simple, clear, and colloquial.* Use contractions. Never use a four- or five-syllable word where two or three shorter ones will do. Write in a style that is more like how you speak, less like how you might write an essay or newspaper article. Ask yourself, "Have I ever used that word in conversation?" If the answer is "No," then replace it.

Tip 4. *Round off large or complex numbers when the exact figure is not vital.* For huge amounts or complicated figures, try to relate the numbers to something that listeners can quickly grasp and retain. For example, area is often given in "football fields," as in "The disputed land is about the size of two football fields." This makes much more sense to a listener than "The disputed land is 247.9 metres by 66.5 metres." Dollar amounts can similarly be manipulated (as long as your arithmetic is reliable), as in "The national debt is now about $17,000 for every man, woman, and child in Canada."

Exercise 3.1

Revise the following eye-oriented sentences (meant to be read silently) to make them ear-oriented (meant to be heard). The content should be clear, easily understood, and memorable *in one hearing*. There are no right and wrong answers, but suggestions on what an ear-oriented version might include begin on page 223.

1. Out of 36,411 eligible voters, only 18,200 actually cast a ballot, with 9,651 votes going to Ms. Miriam Saguchi, 5,927 going to Mr. Vernon Clarke, and 2,620 to Ms. Wendy Grumann, with two ballots spoiled.
2. This month's annual inflation rate is 2.1 percent compared with 2.3 percent last month and 2.7 percent a year ago, with relatively high interest rates of 4.9 percent being given credit for the decline.
3. President and General Manager of Fantastic Products Company Limited, Sheila Moffatt, announced today that the company will be building a new 6,400-square-metre warehouse at the southwest corner of Station St. and First Ave. in our fair city.
4. The perpetrator of the criminal robbery executed an escape via the alternative exit and was chauffeured from the premises by an unknown accomplice driving an opulent sedan that was silver in colour.
5. Gazing across the rooftops, one can observe in the far distance a column of thick, oily, black smoke like a sinister snake uncoiling from its lair and slithering skyward as the chemical plant on the far extreme of the city's outskirts is consumed by flames following this morning's unexplained explosion.

Readability and Credibility

While you are writing for the ears of your listeners when composing broadcast news, there is someone else you have to worry about: the person who is going to read your words on the air. You especially have to worry about this person if it happens to be you; many newscasters write their own copy. A news script that is easy to read with correct emphasis and a conversational flow, one that doesn't cause stumbling or errors, is the goal of good newswriting. Yes, you are writing for the ears of your listeners, and that must be a prime consideration, but you must remember that before it can be heard your material must be read *aloud*.

We will return to the issue of credibility many times in this book. If a newscaster is not credible and authoritative, then listeners will tune in to someone else who is. Imagine a sportscaster who mispronounces the name of a famous hockey or football player. What do sports fans listening to the broadcast think? Obviously, this sportscaster doesn't know the subject, doesn't know anything about the story being read, and can't be relied upon for solid information. The credibility issue is equally important with stumbling, hesitating, or flubbing lines in a newscast. The audience immediately realizes that the person is just reading words off a page and really doesn't know what the story is about. Listeners like to believe that newscasters are experts. They want to believe that they are getting their news from people who know and understand the material. Destroy this belief in any way and you risk losing your listeners.

So you must ensure that your writing is easily readable. Long, complex sentences are hard to read aloud. Tongue twisters are hard to read aloud. Copy that has erasures, stroke-outs, corrections, and other marks is hard to read aloud. Many of the rules and conventions that we will examine in the next chapter have been developed not only to make it easy to write for the ear but also to make it easy for a newscaster to give a flawless read. Following are several considerations apart from those formatting conventions that will make your copy easier to read.

 Tip 1. *Avoid tongue twisters.* Read your copy aloud (softly) before you submit it to ensure that you haven't inadvertently given your newscaster a challenge. It may be obvious that hard-to-pronounce phrases should never be used, but unless you are thinking as a newsreader you can make this error. The following sentence actually came over a broadcast newswire several years ago: "The satellite deployed an umbrella shaped sun shade to protect it from the intense rays of the sun in outer space."

 Tip 2. *Avoid alliteration.* Alliteration is using the same letter or sound in sequence, and it sounds funny on the air. Worse, alliteration with an "s" sound or a hard "b" or "p" will often cause a microphone to rattle or pop.

 Tip 3. *Avoid hard-to-pronounce words.* Even if you can pronounce the words in your head or in rehearsal, the pressure of a newscast can cause horrible problems. Words such as "vehicular" or "incredulity" or "perpetrator" should be avoided. Every newsperson has a "blooper" tape of words that have been booted to hilarious effect; some include these three words and many more that just can't be avoided, such as "psychiatrist" and "Sarajevo." Unfortunately, you never know when a fairly ordinary word or phrase is going to trip a newsreader. All that you can do is make a list of your own hard-to-handle words, and other universally difficult ones, and avoid them in your writing.

 Tip 4. *Use upper- and lower-case letters.* Yes, many news outlets use all upper case, and you may end up working for one that does. However, the beginnings of sentences and proper nouns stand out so much better when upper and lower case are used that, for the sake of the newsreader, this is becoming the favoured style. The following sentences may illustrate the advantages of upper and lower case. Which do you find easier to read without hesitation the first time through?

FISHERIES MINISTER KEVIN EASTMAN HAS JUST ANNOUNCED THE CLO-
SURE OF THE GRAND BANKS FISHERY OFF NEWFOUNDLAND UNTIL
FURTHER NOTICE BECAUSE OF OVERFISHING BY FRENCH AND POR-
TUGUESE TRAWLERS.

Fisheries Minister Kevin Eastman has just announced the closure of the
Grand Banks fishery off Newfoundland until further notice because of
overfishing by French and Portuguese trawlers.

Be guided by your teacher or news director on this one. Some people find
the all-caps format faster and easier to write, but most newsreaders agree
that it's harder to scan.

Exercise 3.2

Rewrite each of these sentences to make it easier to read aloud. Notice the
kinds of things that can throw a reader off track and try to avoid them in your
writing. Suggested answers begin on page 224.

1. The satellite deployed an umbrella shaped sun shade to protect it from
   the intense rays of the sun in outer space.
2. Seconds after sliding safely into second, Cincinnati shortstop Sam
   Chavez stole third.
3. City police report that four people were injured, two seriously, in a five-
   car pileup this morning on the Trans-Canada Highway just west of
   Ninth Street during a snow squall that reduced visibility to near zero
   and caused some sections of the roadway to ice up, raising fears that a
   pileup similar to last year's famous fatal 50-car accident could occur on
   the same stretch of roadway.
4. The Grape and Wine Festival parade took over St. Paul St. in St.
   Catharines today, in a day of celebration of one of the largest of recent
   harvests.
5. The evidence had been recorded on a hidden twin-track tape recorder.

Exercise 3.3

Revise the following eye-oriented paragraphs into ear-oriented writing that is
clear, understandable, and retainable on one hearing. Suggested answers begin
on page 224, but of course yours may differ widely; the important thing is to
apply the principles of writing for the ear discussed above.

1. City councillors voted at their regular Wednesday-night meeting last
   night to increase the annual stipend of a councillor from $21,300 to
   $23,400 next year and to add on $900 the year after, bringing the salary

of a city councillor to $24,300. That is a total raise of $3,000 over two years, or 14.0845 percent. The vote among the councillors was 12 to 7 in favour of giving themselves the increase, with several councillors pointing out that their last raise was almost five years ago.

2. Daniel Cozzini and Estella Lee, both of Edmonton, and co-owners of Hi-Rise Developments Incorporated, announced early this morning at a news conference that they have reached an agreement that has been negotiated over the past 14 months with the city to build a new ten-storey hotel complex in the downtown core area at an estimated cost of $161,455,000. Construction on the new hotel complex will begin next month, and the first phase is scheduled for completion by spring of next year, with a second phase consisting of a shopping plaza, underground parking, and conference facilities, ready within a year after that. The news conference was told that the project will create about 2,000 construction jobs and more than 300 full-time positions when both phases are complete.

3. Assistant Deputy Minister of Industry, Trade, and Tourism, Denise Flemmington, announced this morning that the government will be bringing in legislation sometime in the winter that will permit designated stores in areas of the province with major tourist attractions to begin selling Canadian wines over the counter. She said that strict regulations governing the type of store and the location will be part of the law, which is intended to promote Canadian wine and be a convenience for tourists, but is not to be a liquor outlet in the traditional sense, because the government does not want to undermine the Liquor Control Board.

4. Dennis Mason, the winner of last month's Merritville Speedway Challenge Cup, announced yesterday that he will be building a new car and moving up a category to compete internationally. Mr. Mason was the rookie of the year last year and leads all racers this year in points for the Manitoba Drivers' Championship. The new car will be sponsored by Corntech Racing and built in Winnipeg on a Ford frame by Mason's crew. They hope to have the car ready and tested in time for next year's NASCAR racing season.

5. OTTAWA — The tax burden on individual Canadians and corporations is higher than in any other major industrial country except France, deputy finance minister David Dodge said yesterday. The total of all government taxes — federal, provincial, and municipal — has climbed to almost 40 percent of the gross domestic product, Mr. Dodge said. That means individuals and businesses in Canada paid about $280 billion in taxes last year, based on a GDP of $700 billion. Only France,

with total taxes at about 44 percent of GDP, has a higher tax burden among the world's seven major industrial democracies, he added. Ottawa defines "tax burden" as total taxes paid to federal, provincial, and municipal governments, expressed as a percentage of GDP. — Canadian Press

Assignments

1. Record a newscast on a local radio station. Clip the stories from a local newspaper that correspond to the radio stories you recorded. Compare them in terms of length, complexity, detail, and overall effect.

2. Clip two stories from a newspaper and two from a news magazine. Read through the stories carefully, highlighting any words that you seldom hear in normal conversation. Underline any sentences longer than 50 words.

3. Rewrite these two stories to make them more suitable to be *heard* on a radio or TV newscast.

Unit One
Review Exercises

> ## Review 1.1

Which of the seven news values makes each of these stories newsworthy (there may be two or three)?

1. A major drug company has announced the recall of all bottles of a popular multivitamin because of fears they might have been contaminated.
   news value(s): _____

2. Police are at the scene of a train derailment west of town. No injuries are reported, and the train's cargo is not dangerous.
   news value(s): _____

3. A city councillor has been fined 100 dollars for speeding. Councillor Verne Drennan led the fight at city council to have speed limits in residential areas reduced from 60 kilometres per hour to 50.
   news value(s): _____

4. Thirteen local men face charges after being caught in a police crackdown on prostitution. All are charged with soliciting sex from an undercover police officer.
   news value(s): _____

5. A spring storm sweeping up the Atlantic seaboard has dumped 30 centimetres of snow on Boston, and the weather office says it's headed this way.
   news value(s): _____

6. A strike in Seattle is threatening the supply of electronic components to a local firm. Layoffs are expected next week unless the strike is settled.
   news value(s): _____

7. Thirty-seven residents of Medicine Hat now hold the record for the number of people who could cram themselves into a standard-size telephone booth. All 37 are between the ages of four and six.
   news value(s): _____

8. Fantasydate is a new service in our area that lets computer users get to know each other by reading each other's fantasies anonymously via computer link-up before exchanging phone numbers. In other cities, it's already a multimillion-dollar business.
   news value(s): _____

9. City council last night approved two new snow-removal vehicles for the Public Works Department at a total cost of over 150 thousand dollars.
   news value(s): _____

10. New studies released by the United Nations suggest that levels of ultra-violet radiation from the sun may reach record proportions this summer as the ozone layer is again beginning to thin.
news value(s): _____

Review 1.2

Select six of the stories from Review Exercise 1.1 for inclusion in a newscast and arrange them in an appropriate order. *Note:* taped inserts are available for stories 1, 5, 7, and 8.

Assignment

Request permission to spend a shift as an observer in the newsroom of a local station. Record your impressions, and write a report based on the following guidelines.

1. Note the story lineup for three consecutive newscasts. Account for differences from hour to hour, and consider why some stories did not change position.
2. Note the source for each story broadcast during the shift, and draw conclusions about this station's news sources and policies.
3. Draw conclusions about the station's demographics (audience) and policies.

UNIT 2

Writing the News

Broadcast Writing Conventions

In the previous chapter, we began to explore how we must adapt our writing skills to the peculiar requirements of broadcast media. Over the years, many rules and formats have been adopted that are designed to make the words on the page both easier to hear and understand for a listener and easier to read aloud without error for a reader. In this chapter, those rules and format conventions are presented. At the end of the chapter is a list of these points to refer to as you write your stories.

Numbers and Symbols

You are at the news desk, the microphone is live, and you are about halfway through the newscast when the following sentence appears: "The budget surplus is now estimated to be $45,455,699,701, an increase of almost $9,000,000,000 from original estimates that were made last spring." Can you read it correctly without hesitation the first time you see it? Unlikely. For this reason, a generally accepted convention has been devised.

- All numbers from zero to eleven are written out in words.
- Numbers from 12 to 999 are written as numerals. Ordinal numbers usually follow the same rule as other numbers (sixth, eleventh, but 45th and 101st).
- "Thousand," "million," "billion," et cetera, are written out ("hundred" is never written out unless you want your reader to say "12 hundred" instead of "one thousand 200").
- All symbols are written out ($ is dollars, % is percent, .4 is point [or decimal] four, a.m. is morning, p.m. is afternoon or evening, etc.).
- All fractions are written out (1/2 is one-half, 4/5 is four-fifths, etc.)

Exceptions:

- Times appear in numerals (10 in the morning instead of ten).
- Years also appear in numerals (1995 is acceptable).
- Sports scores are normally written as numerals (7–6, 24–7, etc.).
- Numbers that begin a sentence and the number 111 are written out.

So, presuming that exact numbers are needed and rounding them off would damage the stories, here are some examples of how broadcast copy would handle numbers.

"$4,697.77" becomes "four thousand 697 dollars and 77 cents."

"66.6%" becomes "66 point six percent."

"1,450,000" becomes "one million, 450 thousand."

Exercise 4.1

Rewrite each of the following into correct broadcast style. In each case, assume the exact number is needed in the story (but always keep in mind that, where exact numbers are not required, you should round them off). Answers begin on page 225.

1. $4,567,909
2. today at 7:00 p.m.
3. 794.5
4. $4.95
5. 9%
6. 11,565,000
7. 371
8. 7 3/4
9. 111.9
10. $604,411.04

Abbreviations and Acronyms

Just as numbers on a page can be confusing, abbreviations or acronyms can easily be misread. Just to be safe, it is standard practice to write out any short forms such as Inc. or Ltd. or Cel. (for Celsius) or Cdn. or St. for saint or street or the names of provinces.

Listeners do not always have the specialized knowledge that would enable them to figure out uncommon acronyms or initials. Common ones such as RCMP and U.N., NHL and CFL, U.S.A. and NATO are acceptable. But write out the full name of an organization when there is any suspicion that your listeners may not understand the acronym. After your first use of the full name, you may want to use the acronym on subsequent mentions if you think your listeners will "get it" without any trouble.

Some news directors prefer hyphens between the letters in initials (U-S-A and R-C-M-P) to make them easier to read accurately. Be guided by the usage in your classroom or newsroom.

Exercise 4.2

Use your judgement of what would be both clearly understandable to listeners and easily readable by the newscaster to rewrite each of the following into correct broadcast format. Suggested answers begin on page 225.

1. St. John's mayor, Kevin Murphy, has worked for Sysco Ltd. since 1992.
2. Canada was a charter member of NATO and has more recently joined O-A-S. (NATO: North Atlantic Treaty Organization; O-A-S: Organization of American States)
3. The wanted man fled St. Thomas, Ont., and was later seen in Pt. Alberni, B.C., where he was picked up by the R-C-M-P. (R-C-M-P: Royal Canadian Mounted Police)
4. The United States of America (USA) is trying to get an agreement on agriculture at the General Agreement on Tariffs and Trade (GATT) talks going on in St. John's, Nfld.
5. The Canadian Radio, Television and Telecommunications Commission (CRTC) has granted an extension to the licence of the Canadian Broadcasting Corporation (CBC).
6. A report from the Canadian Security and Intelligence Service (CSIS) says that the Gov. General of Canada and the Lt. Gov. of Alta. were under surveillance by the Central Intelligence Agency (CIA) during a period in the mid-nineteen sixties.
7. The United Autoworkers Union (UAW) and the New Democratic Party (NDP) have different views on how to handle the question of layoffs at G-M Inc. in St. Catharines, Ont. (G-M: General Motors)
8. Three people have been rushed to Colson Mem. Hosp. after a three-car collision on Windsor Ave. at Dawson Dr. this morning.
9. N.W. winds of 30 kph will swing to the N.E. and pick up 12 or 15 km in strength by this afternoon.

10. Gen. Mackenzie and Lt. White will speak at the C-A-B convention in Ft. Lauderdale, Fla., about the media's role in United Nations (U.N.) peacekeeping operations.
(C-A-B: Canadian Association of Broadcasters)

Names, Addresses, Titles, Race, Age

As a general rule, give the first and last name of a person in the news on the first mention. After that, refer to the person by last name only unless the person is a child, in which case it is more appropriate to use the first name on the second and subsequent mentions.

> The arrested woman is Denise Jourdan of Winnipeg. Jourdan will appear in provincial court for a bail hearing. . . .

> Little Vic Perroni is lucky to be alive. Vic, who is four, was playing near a storm sewer at North Street last night when. . . .

Addresses are given only when the people involved are local, and you might expect your listeners to want to know "Was he my neighbour?" "Which Jack Smith? The one who works with my husband?" "Did the holdup (accident, incident) happen in my neighbourhood?" It is particularly important to give addresses in smaller-market stations, for there is a greater likelihood that listeners will know many of the people in their community. Many stations choose not to broadcast street numbers for privacy and security reasons.

> The injured man is Jules Bastien of Maple Street.

> A local man is one million dollars richer tonight, thanks to the provincial lottery. Reza Mahoud of Parkway Drive didn't even check his ticket in Thursday's draw until. . . .

Titles such as Mr., Mrs., and Ms. are not used in broadcast stories unless there is an intention to confer respect or dignity on the person. Then a title is used after the first mention of the name instead of using the last name alone.

> Irish President Mary Harper has praised the early Irish settlers in this area as people who were willing to endure hardships so that their children

could have better lives. Ms. Harper was in town this morning to meet the mayor and other dignitaries while on a two-week tour of Canada. . . .

Ninety-seven-year-old Erik Olafsen, who flew with the RCAF during the Second World War, placed a wreath at the cenotaph. Mr. Olafsen paid tribute to those. . . .

Cumbersome and lengthy official titles should be shortened whenever possible. There is no formula for doing so correctly, but it is easy to make enquiries to find out the proper forms for short titles if you aren't sure. For example, The Right Honourable Gaston Tanguay, Minister of Defence, is easily condensed to Defence Minister Gaston Tanguay. However, be sure that your shortened version is correct. Some officials are extremely prickly about their titles and have been known to correct reporters thoroughly and publicly when they have felt slighted. Note that judges are named "Mister Justice (full name)" or "Madam Justice (full name)" on the first mention, and "Judge (last name)" on subsequent mentions.

Race should not be a part of any broadcast story unless the story's meaning clearly requires it. When you're not sure whether you should include race, ask yourself, "Would I be identifying the race of this person if he was Scottish or Swedish?" If not, then there is no justification for mentioning race. Here are parts of two stories in which race *is* part of the context and can be used.

. . . Mr. Singh was the first Sikh to hold the office of mayor in a Canadian city.

The winner in the poetry competition, Jian Yang, is a Chinese immigrant who has been speaking English for only six years.

Age, like race, should be included only if the nature of the story requires it. A child's age is frequently used because it is often an integral part of the story.

. . . The Dicksons' five-year-old son Jeffrey received only minor injuries.

If the age of the person involved is an unusual or significant part of what happened, then it is necessary to include it. Otherwise, it adds nothing, so leave it out. In the following instances, age is justifiably mentioned.

An 81-year-old grandmother is in the graduating class at Sir John A. Macdonald Secondary School today. Mrs. Lily Pearson returned to school. . . .

The armed holdup was the work of two 12-year-olds.

Attribution and Quotation

Attribution means giving the source of information, and it is a requirement of responsible reporting. You can't say "The police budget this year is completely inadequate" without attributing this opinion to someone: "Police Chief Donald Barnes says the police budget this year is completely inadequate." Attribution is necessary whenever

- the facts in the story are questionable;
- opinion or controversial material is included; and
- the source of the story is a necessary part of the information.

Here are examples in which attribution is a must. Without it, these sentences are unacceptable for broadcast.

A seven-year-old Russian girl has given birth to a baby boy.

The death penalty is the only appropriate punishment for this crime.

The strike at City Hall will be over by noon tomorrow.

With attribution, these sentences can be used on air.

According to a Reuters News report, a seven-year-old Russian girl. . . .

The mother of the victim told reporters that the death penalty is the only. . . .

According to the union negotiator, the strike at City Hall will be over . . . .

Attribution is not necessary when the facts of the story are easily verified, their source is obvious, and they contain no opinion. Attributing material that is clearly factual can become clumsy and boring. No attribution is necessary for this item:

Canada Day celebrations are scheduled for Water Park at 6:30 this evening, with fireworks and a brass band as part of the entertainment.

In print, attribution usually follows the information, as in

The arrested man fired two shots at the officers, according to the police report.

In broadcast, however, this approach can be confusing to a listener who may miss the attribution or think that it is part of the next sentence. Therefore, in radio and TV news scripts, attribution comes first.

According to the police report, the arrested man fired two shots at the officers.

Since we are discussing attribution, this is a good time to mention quotation. Quotations are an important part of newspaper stories, giving the exact words spoken by a participant in the event that the story is about. In broadcast, however, the exact words of the participant should be on tape, not repeated by a newscaster. Try to avoid direct quotation; instead paraphrase what was said. The reason for doing so should be obvious: listeners cannot hear quotation marks. For a newscaster to have to say "quote" and "unquote" is terribly awkward and complicates the listener's already difficult task of getting the information on one hearing. Avoid saying

The coach said, and I quote, They whipped us good, unquote.

Instead, use

The coach said that his team had received a whipping from the Hornets.

Punctuation

Punctuation in written English is used as a signal to the reader how the material is to be read. Commas indicate a pause, exclamation points show emphasis, periods suggest the end of a complete thought, colons signal that an example or list is about to follow, and so on. In broadcast, the voice provides the emphasis and inflection that add meaning, colour, and interest to the words. Broadcast punctuation, therefore, has been modified to aid the reader, whose voice will be heard.

- Periods and capital letters to signal the end of one sentence and the start of another are retained.
- Colons and semicolons are usually not used at all.
- Commas may be used to separate items in a list or to indicate insignificant pauses.

Major pauses in a sentence are indicated by ellipses (. . .), as in "Following his acquittal, Sullivan . . . who had already spent two weeks in prison while awaiting trial . . . was released." Don't overuse ellipses, however, because every reader has a different approach and rhythm. By telling the reader when to pause, you are limiting that individual style. Use ellipses only when there *must* be a pause for the sentence to make sense. Readers will always mark up their copy anyway, indicating with slashes and other symbols (see Chapter 12) how to approach the story.

Pronouncers

A "pronouncer" is a phonetic spelling of a difficult word or an uncommon name, and it is used to assist a newsreader in getting the right pronunciation during the newscast. A pronouncer appears in square brackets immediately after the difficult word or name. It is divided into syllables, with the syllable that is emphasized written in full caps.

> Local Member of Parliament Gordon Liebowiktz [LEE bow wits] says the new initiatives will create jobs in this region.

It is especially important that the names of local people and places in the news are pronounced correctly, since all listeners are going to know when a mistake has been made — and a mistake on the name of a well-known local figure instantly destroys the newscaster's credibility. Never guess at a pronunciation. Find it out, even if it means phoning to confirm a correct emphasis. Most stations keep lists of local names with their correct pronunciations posted in the newsrooms, and wire services periodically send out pronunciation guides for difficult Canadian and foreign names; these, too, should be posted.

Exercise 4.3

Practise writing pronouncers by providing them for these well-known names and places. Don't forget to indicate where the emphasis goes by capitalizing that syllable, and, if you don't know the correct pronunciation, *find it out*. Answers begin on page 226. Example: Susan Gelinas [JELL-ee-na].

1. Patrick Roy (hockey player)
2. Michael Ondaatje (writer)
3. Sarajevo
4. Antonio Vivaldi
5. Galapagos Islands

Exercise 4.4

Collect the names of ten local personalities who might be in the news (politicians, sports figures, union leaders, heads of organizations, prominent religious, business, or social leaders, etc.), and provide a pronouncer for each.

Correct the following sentences for use as broadcast copy, following the standard conventions and formats outlined above. Suggested answers begin on page 226.

1. The new mayor is Mrs. Cynthia Boyko, 48, who has served on city council for 7 years, representing the Broadway Dr. and Clager St. district.

2. "Men must solve the problem of violence against women," says Mary Gallagher, 34, who is Ojibway and a member of the provincial task force studying the problem.

3. According to a spokesperson for Northern Industries Co. Ltd., company profits fell .5% last year, resulting in the planned layoffs.

4. Officers from the M-N-R were called in to check the animal for rabies after it attacked 26-year-old Mr. John Spodafori. (M-N-R: Ministry of Natural Resources)

5. The Sask. Min. of Ag. says that "Canada must not give in to the Europeans and destroy our supply management system of agricultural marketing."

6. The new 3.6% tax increase is expected to raise an additional $45,700 for the city treasury, cutting into last year's $21,564 deficit, according to village treasurer Mrs. Nancy West.

7. The Stallions, in the playoffs for the first time in 6 yrs., need a good performance from their rookie goaltender, Marc Dupuis.

8. A county P-T-A meeting at 6 p.m. tonight will debate the "1/2 week" proposal suggested by the teachers' union. (P-T-A: Parent–Teacher Association)

9. At about 6 a.m. a man entered the convenience store on St. James Ave. and, flashing a hunting knife, demanded money, according to police.

10. The fed. gov't. is increasing the amount of $ paid in transfer fees to the provinces; that's good news for P-E-I's finance minister, Wilson Deng, who is of Chinese ancestry. (P-E-I: Prince Edward Island)

As a final test of your ability to write correctly formatted broadcast copy, use the following facts to write a short story. Suggested answers begin on page 226.

1. • A high-speed chase along Niagara St. and Hwy. 145 occurred last night at about 2 a.m.
   • Police arrested Fredrick Schleich, 26, of 456 Dundas Ave.
   • A cop says "Speeds of over 120 kph were necessary to catch the suspect car."

2. • The local Lions Club fundraiser achieved its goal of $12,500 in just over 6 weeks.

- The money will be used to buy a seeing-eye dog for Tabatha Moul-lambasi, an 8-year-old refugee from the war in Somalia who was blinded by a bullet.

3. • The city's Youth Orchestra will travel to St. Petersburg, Russia, this summer.
   • A grant from Telecomp Co. Inc. makes the trip possible for the 38-member group, aged 9 to 21.
   • Orchestra leader Ms. Regina Dunworthy says "It's the opportunity of a lifetime for these young people."

4. • A local man, Ted Dykstra, 56, is suing his doctor for $1,000,000 in damages for an operation that he says was botched.
   • Dr. Renatta Yager did a facelift for Ted 3 months ago.
   • Ted says "My skin is now so tight I can't close my eyes."

5. • 2 people are dead and 3 are in County Gen. Hosp. with serious injuries.
   • The accident happened early this am on Harwell St., involving 2 vehicles.
   • Mrs. Judith Ryker, 36, and her husband, Kevin, 35, were killed, and their daughter, Cindy, 7, is among the injured. They lived at 456 Harwell St.
   • The people in the other car were Don and Ingrid Belcaster of 78 Porter St., Miami, Fla., both 57.

Assignments

1. Clip three short newspaper stories and rewrite them for on-air use.
2. Write a story that makes as many of the errors mentioned in this chapter as possible. Exchange stories with a colleague for correction.
3. Write a paragraph outlining what happened to you today. Now rewrite the paragraph as a news story, following all the guidelines and conventions in Chapters 3 and 4.

Basic Broadcast Style Checker

NUMBERS

- Write out one to eleven.
- Use numerals for 12 to 999.
- Write out thousand, million, and billion but seldom hundred.
- Round off numbers where possible.

ABBREVIATIONS

- Avoid all abbreviations, including a.m. and p.m.

INITIALS AND ACRONYMS

- Use initials of commonly known organizations (U-N, U-S-A, NATO, N-D-P).
- Spell out others.

NAMES AND TITLES

- Use first and last name on the first mention.
- Use last name only on all subsequent mentions (except for children).
- Mr., Mrs., and Ms. are used rarely and only to show respect.

RACE AND AGE

- Avoid any mention of either unless it is necessary to the story.

ATTRIBUTION AND QUOTATION

- Avoid direct quotation; paraphrase what was said.
- Give the attribution before the information.
- Attribute when information is controversial or opinion, facts are doubtful, or source is necessary.

PUNCTUATION

- Use . . . (ellipses) to indicate a major pause necessary for listeners to understand.
- Use , (comma) for items in a list and for minor and optional pauses.

PRONOUNCER

- Use [ ] (square brackets) for phonetic spelling, with the word broken into syllables and capital letters to indicate emphasis.

The Lead

Writing the Lead

The lead is the first sentence of the news script. It is also the most important sentence in the script because, in addition to providing information (which every sentence in the story must do), it must give some idea of what the story is about, and it must attract the listener's interest. The lead has the same function in radio and television stories as the headline has in newspaper writing. There are several different types of lead sentences, some more effective and useful than others. Let's look at the basics of how to write a lead first.

KEEP IT SHORT AND SIMPLE

A lead sentence more than any other in the story should be short and simple. A long, complex sentence with too much information in it will be lost on the listener. It is unfair to expect listeners to begin paying attention to facts, figures, and details right from the sound of the reader's voice. No, listeners must be warmed up, attracted to the story by the essence of what makes it interesting; then they will tune in to the details.

GIVE INFORMATION

While the lead is an attention-getter, it should also provide information about the story — in most cases, the most important and urgent element of the story. In other words, it is not enough to use attention-getting gimmicks in the lead; listeners soon grow tired of such tricks. We have all heard of the classified ad (and many of us have tried variations on it) that says "SEX! Now that I have attracted your attention, how would you like to buy an almost new couch?" That strategy may work once, but it becomes irritating when it's used again. The best way to attract listeners is to tell them what is interesting about the story they are about to hear.

A common error for beginners is to use the words *happened* or *occurred* in their leads. Avoid using those words. That you are reporting the story makes it obvious that it "happened," so to say so is redundant, as in "A plane crash happened in China this morning." Instead, give information about the incident. "A plane crash in China this morning is being investigated for possible sabotage."

MAKE IT IMMEDIATE

One of the advantages that broadcast news has over newspapers is that it can be immediate. Stories can be relayed to a listener as they unfold. This is one of the main reasons that people want news on radio and television — to get it quickly, to hear or see it first. To make good use of this natural advantage, indicate as much as possible the immediacy of your story. The lead is the natural place to do so. The verb in your lead should be in the present, not the past, tense. Ask yourself "What is happening *in the present* (right now!) in this story?"

Here's an example. There was an accident this morning at a busy intersection. Two local residents were killed. An inexperienced writer might lead with "There was a car accident this morning that killed two local people." The rookie has told listeners that this is old news: "There *was. . . .*" Even though he added that it occurred this morning, he lessened the impact of the story by taking away its immediacy. A much more effective lead would be "Two local people are dead after a car accident this morning" or "Police are investigating a fatal car accident." We have put the present element of this story up front, where it can have the impact that will grab the attention of our listeners. We are telling them what is happening right now, as they are listening!

Finding a present element is not always easy and requires practice; however, every story has a present element, or it shouldn't be on the air! Here are a few more examples of making the lead immediate by including the story's present element.

Past: The mayor of Regina resigned last night.

Present: Regina is without a mayor.
　　　　　The search is on for a new mayor in Regina.

Past: Police arrested a man in connection with the robberies that have been plaguing Waterport convenience stores.

Present: A man is under arrest in connection with the robberies. . . .
Police are holding a suspect in the robberies. . . .

Past: The local blood drive reached its goal a day early.

Present: Blood drive organizers are thrilled. . . .
The local blood drive is over. . . . and it has been a success.

This is a very important concept. Ask yourself whenever you are assembling the facts of a story "What is going on *right now* in this story?" Chances are that the answer to that question will supply your lead.

Exercise 5.1

Write a lead that expresses the present element in each of these stories. Remember to keep the lead short and to give information. Suggested answers begin on page 227.

1. • The space shuttle *Pegasus* landed safely this morning at Cape Canaveral, Florida.
   • The eight astronauts, who performed more than 60 experiments without a hitch during the ten-day mission, have been sent home to rest.
2. • Fifty Canadian soldiers arrived home to Halifax last night from their peacekeeping mission with the United Nations in the Middle East.
   • They have been away for six months and will be replaced by Swedish troops.
3. • Parliament passed a bill today that is designed to encourage small businesses to hire young people who have never held full-time jobs before.
   • The law will provide 50 million dollars in salaries and benefits, which the businesses can apply for when they hire workers who qualify for the program.
4. • An avalanche in the Swiss Alps killed four tourists yesterday, including a Canadian whose name has not been released.
   • The four were on a mountain-climbing expedition with 12 others when the accident occurred. Two more people have not been found.
5. • Mayor Diane Lewicki announced at a news conference this morning that she will be a candidate in the provincial by-election coming up in April.

• She served two terms as mayor and ran unsuccessfully once before for the legislature. She will run for the Liberals. No other parties have announced candidates yet.

Another way to provide immediacy when the simple present tense is inappropriate, or to add variety to your leads, is to use the present-perfect tense. This means adding the helper verb *have* or *has* to the past tense of the verb you want to use. The effect is to bring an event into the present and give it the immediacy you want in a lead.

Past tense: Union negotiators agreed to a settlement late last night.

Present-perfect tense: Union negotiators *have agreed* to a settlement in their wage dispute.

Past tense: The Nobel prize for chemistry was awarded today to a Canadian.

Present-perfect tense: The Nobel prize for chemistry *has been* awarded to a Canadian.

Exercise 5.2

Change these past-tense leads into leads in the present-perfect tense. Answers begin on page 227.

1. A Speelton woman was killed in a car accident.
2. A teacher at Confederation High School won a marathon race in Japan.
3. Aid workers in Somalia received a shipment of medical supplies and food.
4. Retailers had the best Christmas in ten years, according to the Better Business Bureau.
5. Parliament adjourned for the summer recess with several issues unresolved.

STIMULATE INTEREST

In newspaper writing, a headline performs the same function as the lead in a broadcast story. In fact, it does a much better job, since it can be in bold type, even in colour, varying in size with the importance of the story, and thereby attract readers to the story underneath. You must do likewise with the first sentence of your story. Think of the lead as a headline for the ears. By leading with an important present element, you will stimulate the interest of your audience. However, there are several common errors to avoid to ensure that interest is maintained in your lead sentence.

 Tip 1. *Never lead with a name that is unfamiliar to your audience.* No matter how interesting the story, you will lose your audience by the time you get to the good stuff if you begin with the name of someone they don't know and don't yet care about.

> Timothy Duff of Main Street is in critical condition in City General after. . . .

By the time you tell the story about this tragedy, no one is listening. If you want to keep your audience hooked, give them information that will catch their attention — don't turn them away.

 Tip 2. *Don't lead with complex numbers or complicated facts.* If they are necessary to the story, then save them for later, and let your lead sketch out the information that is important.

> The two million, 600 thousand dollars paid by the city art gallery for a sketch by Tom Thomson is a record.

By the time listeners have caught on to what is interesting about this story, they have forgotten the number because they weren't interested in it when it was first read — it didn't mean anything then. Instead, let the numbers come later:

> A sketch bought by the city art gallery is a record breaker. The drawing . . . by Tom Thomson . . . cost the gallery two million, 600 thousand dollars.

Now the lead attracts interest, and the number has impact.

Exercise 5.3

Correct these weak leads by applying the methods discussed above. Answers begin on page 227.

1. A knifing happened outside a Main Street bar last night, and a local teenager was badly hurt.
2. A four-percent raise over two years with an option for another two percent in the third year is the settlement that unionized workers for the city were offered last night after negotiating for almost 14 hours.

3. Snow-removal crews finally got the city streets clear in time for rush hour after our 30-centimetre snowfall last night.

4. Thelma Jacobson of Superior Street is the proud mother of quadruplets this morning.

5. At 2:30 this morning, a minor earthquake woke many city residents, but no damage or injuries were reported.

6. A ferry capsized in Panama yesterday, and the number of dead was estimated at 40, with more than 20 people still missing.

7. An alert guard dog is credited with saving the lives of a High Street family when their house burned to the ground last night because of faulty wiring in a string of Christmas tree lights that ignited the tree, and the fire quickly spread to the kitchen before engulfing the entire house in flames.

8. A local priest . . . well known for his community activity . . . was found dead of a heart attack.

9. A strike has occurred at the Tinman Foundry.

10. Three thousand, 600 dollars was cut from the police budget at last night's City Financial Committee meeting.

Types of Leads

THE HARD LEAD

This is the kind of lead we have been discussing up to now. It presents the main, immediate element of the story in a compact, powerful statement. It is the most common broadcast lead and should be the one you use most often.

THE SOFT OR FEATURE LEAD

For a story that is lighter or longer than most, a soft lead is appropriate. This may be a news story that provides background or presents an interesting character but is not immediate or urgent. A soft lead is meant to be intriguing, to set the scene for a light or leisurely telling of the story, and it does not have to follow the rules set down for a hard lead.

> They say that the exception proves the rule. Well, a local businesswoman has gone a long way to demonstrate the truth of that statement. When Merle Margolis started her plastics business three years ago, she was told that. . . .

Most parents dream of a son who will be an NHL star or a major-league baseball player. Not so Jan and Raj Amritsar. They recognized their boy's musical genius early, and now their confidence is turning into an international recording career for son David. . . .

Notice in both of these examples that the leads are in the present tense but do not provide hard information. They're intriguing and attention-getting without telling us what the story is about. These are soft leads.

THE QUESTION LEAD

There are several reasons to avoid question leads. They are overused. They are cute. They are tough for a newscaster, who has to phrase them just right and get across a new tone of voice. They can easily be confused for a commercial. They invite listeners to respond negatively. A question lead is a type of soft lead (it would never be used in a hard-hitting story) that might be used (very rarely) to begin a light story.

Did you ever wonder whether the French really are better lovers? Well, a new survey on the sex lives of French men and women reveals. . . .

THE STATEMENT LEAD

This is another one to avoid. A statement lead begins the story with a dramatic quotation or statement from someone without telling listeners who made the comment. The result is that it sounds as if the newscaster is making the outrageous statement, and it certainly can prick up a listener's ears! But the impact is almost always quickly lost when listeners realize they have been tricked or confused.

The prime minister is a liar and a cheat. This opinion was expressed today by the leader of the opposition, who was speaking to a convention. . . .

The current state of the local dog pound is atrocious . . . according to the outgoing director of the Humane Society, who is resigning in protest over conditions at the facility.

THE FRAGMENT OR HEADLINE LEAD

Some stations permit fragment leads. They copy the style of newspaper headlines — short, dramatic phrases that are not complete sentences (sentence fragments).

New career for hairdresser. William Kittering has been successful in his first try for election to city council. Kittering, a hairdresser for the past eleven years. . . .

High-speed chase ends in death. Two local teens are dead after their vehicle overturned while they were being chased by provincial police. A police spokesperson. . . .

A fragment lead follows all the same principles as the other leads: it must be short, informative, immediate, and interesting. The only difference is that some verbs and articles (*the*, *an*, *a*) are left out in imitation of newspaper headlines (which are shortened to fit available space on a page).

Fragment leads are not conversational (no one speaks this way), and they are an awkward, strange-sounding holdover from the days when newscasts consisted of deep-voiced men reading the daily newspaper into a radio microphone. However, some stations continue to use them. Because this kind of lead is easy to write, and because many news directors won't allow them, beginning newswriters are advised to practise full-sentence leads and avoid using fragment leads.

Exercise 5.4

Improve these leads. Check your answers against those beginning on page 228.

1. A Canadian wine company won a gold medal at a competition in France.
2. According to the latest industry statistics, microbreweries account for about one percent of the beer sold in Canada, with Molson's and Labatt's sharing about 93 percent and small, regional breweries taking four percent.
3. Schoolteachers are overpaid and underworked according to the head of a school board in southern Alberta.
4. Mrs. Josie Vansickle is in serious condition in hospital after being struck in a hit-and-run accident this morning.
5. There was a scuffle on the picket line at Memorial Enterprises this morning. Two people were arrested. . . .
6. Hurricane Dennis swept in on the coast of South Carolina this morning and caused four deaths and more than ten million dollars in property damage before continuing up the coast to North Carolina.
7. How many town councillors does it take to change a light bulb? Well, it will soon take fewer if a measure to reduce the number of councillors is passed this evening.

8. Perfectly OK, just fine. That's the way Mayor Trillman described his health this morning after returning home from hospital following his triple-bypass surgery on the weekend.

9. Two boys missing in the woods north of Clearwater were found unharmed and in good shape after a three-day search.

10. Sexual assault charges were brought against a Windsor man after complaints from four of his employees and a three-week police investigation.

Exercise 5.5

Write the leads for stories on the following sets of facts. Don't forget to use correct broadcast conventions and formats in writing your leads. Compare your answers with the suggestions beginning on page 228.

1. • Coffee producers announced today that coffee bean prices would rise 20% starting in the new year.

   • The rise is the result of poor harvests caused by rainy, cold weather over much of South America.

2. • A man found guilty of 9 counts of break and enter was sentenced to 2 years by Judge Patricia Veray.

   • Stanley Price was found guilty two weeks ago and still faces trial on fraud and extortion charges.

3. • Councillor Devon McMillan called a news conference today to complain about city council's budget process.

   • He said that all the power for budget changes is in the hands of long-time councillors on the Finance Committee and that newcomers like him are not listened to.

4. • A transport truck, westbound on Highway 18, collided head-on with a car going east at 7 this morning. The highway was blocked for three hours.

   • All three passengers in the car were killed. The truck driver was sent to hospital with a broken leg. No names have been released, but the car had New Brunswick plates.

5. • A local company just won a multimillion-dollar contract to supply shoes to the Canadian army. It could mean 20 jobs over the three years of the contract.

   • Footpad Inc. was on the verge of bankruptcy only two years ago, but new owners turned it around by getting government work and specializing in hiking boots.

Assignments

1. Record and transcribe (write out) the leads from each story of a newscast. Identify the type of lead and critique it based on the information provided here. Improve them if you can.
2. Write broadcast leads for five newspaper stories from a recent edition of a local paper.
3. Write five leads that deliberately violate as many of the rules about leads as possible. Exchange them with a colleague for correction.

6

Building the Story

The overriding principle in news writing for broadcast is "tell a story." While broadcast news is a great deal more formal and structured than gossip or conversation or joke-telling, it follows in the same oral tradition. Some radio newswriters begin every story by picturing a friend or acquaintance and asking, "Hey, have you heard . . . ?" Doing so keeps them firmly on track with the conversational and personal style and structure appropriate to broadcast. (It also helps them to write a really good, attention-getting lead.) All good storytellers know that successful stories have a beginning, a middle, and an ending. Let's begin at the beginning.

Support the Lead

The lead is the foundation upon which the rest of the story must be constructed. The sentence after the lead must support the lead, providing whatever details are necessary so that the audience will understand the main idea of the story. The lead, remember, is only an introduction, an attention-getter, and usually omits detail in order to convey the immediacy and importance of the story. The next sentence fills in the gaps.

Lead: A local woman is going to jail for two years.

Next sentence: Vera Purvis was sentenced this afternoon for her part in the 1994 robbery of a gas station in Clearwater.

Lead: There will be no increase in municipal taxes next year.

Next sentence: City council last night voted down a proposed five-per-cent tax hike and instructed the Finance Committee to come up with a new budget holding taxes to last year's level.

Promises made in the lead, or expectations raised, must be satisfied quickly. In the story above, for example, it would be wrong to follow the lead with a chronological account of last night's council meeting. Tax increases have been mentioned in the lead, and they must be explained in the next sentence. In most cases, the first two sentences would make a complete (though short and undetailed) story, leaving a listener with sufficient information to understand the basics of the event. The second sentence is the key, filling in the gaps left by the attention-getting lead.

Answer Your Audience's Questions

The ability to put yourself in the place of your audience is one of the most important skills you can develop as a newswriter. What about this story will your audience want to know? need to know? Normally, the lead answers the question "What is happening?" The second sentence fills out the information in the lead. From there, facts should be added that will answer the basic questions "Who, what, where, when, why, and how?" Often the lead and the supporting sentence will cover many of these questions, leaving only a few loose ends to tie up in the following sentences.

Never pad a story with unnecessary information. At the same time though, make sure that any important questions your audience may have are answered. Broadcast news stories are short and should not be allowed to bog down with irrelevant or unimportant details. Radio and TV newswriters must put up with the criticism that they are superficial, over-simplifying complex issues; the fact is, listeners and viewers cannot absorb complex details or complicated explanations when they hear the information only once, read at a normal conversational speed. Most stories consist of the lead, supporting information, and one or two additional facts, and they are about 20 to 30 seconds long (excluding any audio- or videotape). Select the facts that need to be in the story by applying the news values discussed in Chapter 1 and by using your knowledge of your audience to gauge which facts and details will be important to them. Of course, audiences are different from station to station, and the information selected for broadcast by one newswriter may well differ from that chosen by another, based on each writer's perception of the needs of that station's audience (see Chapter 14: "Station Style").

Flow

A good news story is not a random list of facts. The facts should relate clearly to one another and be assembled in such a way that there is "flow" or continuity. Sometimes this means that facts are presented in climactic order, with the lead containing the most important fact and then the rest of the information following in descending order of importance. This is called the "inverted pyramid" method of writing and is the standard for newspaper writing because it makes it easy for an editor to cut a story to fit the space available on the page, knowing that less important facts are near the end. In broadcast, it is only one possible way of telling a story. It is more important that the story is unified, that it sounds like a story, not a recitation of unrelated facts. To achieve this effect, the items in the story must be carefully considered for their relationship to each other so that one flows from the preceding item and leads clearly to the next. Selective use of transitional words in the story can also help to give it a sense of unity. Such words include *and, but, however, so, in addition, while, furthermore, then, when, yet, plus*, and so on.

Ending

The last sentence in the story is the second most important after the lead. It is the sentence that audiences hear last and are most likely to retain. Broadcast news is impermanent and quickly forgotten, so a good last sentence will recall the main element in the story and close the piece with impact. This does not mean that an important fact should be withheld so that you can close with a bang. Rather, the final sentence should recall the main element of the story while adding something that either puts the story in perspective or suggests where the events just described might head in the future. In the story above about city council rejecting a tax increase, the final line might read as follows.

> Last week the Chair of the Finance Committee . . . Gina Walters . . . threatened to resign if her committee's recommendation was not accepted by council.

or

> If the budget is held to last year's level, this will be the third year in a row that residents have had no increase in property taxes.

or

> The decision by council follows two weeks of presentations and demonstrations in council and committee meetings by a coalition of antitax organizations that demanded this year's spending be held to last year's level.

Any of these three endings would give perspective and context to the facts of the story, bringing the listener into the picture more fully about why this story is important, or why it is interesting, or how it may continue to unfold, while at the same time recalling the story's main theme.

Summary

In a very short time (20 to 30 seconds, only four or five sentences), the newswriter tries to tell a story that will capture the interest of the audience. The first sentence is the lead. The second sentence supports the lead, clarifying and answering questions raised in the lead. The body of the story adds further information (normally, not more than two additional important facts) while maintaining the unity or flow of the story. Careful selection of facts for continuity and news value as well as thoughtful ordering of these facts and the use of transitions will produce a well-structured story. The last line recalls the most important idea of the story while adding perspective and impact.

Not every story accomplishes all this in the same way; this chapter is not meant to provide a formula that will churn out stories all sounding the same. However, a skilful broadcast writer will include all the elements described here while telling each story to highlight its unique value and interest to the audience.

Exercise 6.1

Write a well-crafted, 25-second news story from the following set of facts. Don't forget to spend extra time to create an effective lead, support the lead, give the story flow, and end with impact. You are writing for an early-morning newscast. A suggested version begins on page 228.

- A fire alarm was turned in to Fire Station Number Six (corner of 1st and Fraser) this morning at 6.
- Firefighters rushed to the scene, 1567 Purvis Ave., a single-family dwelling.
- The house was engulfed in flames when they arrived, and they radioed for help from Stations Two and Seven.
- The fire has not yet been brought under control, and the homes on either side of it have been evacuated as a precaution.
- 1567 Purvis Ave. is owned by Vern and Sarah Welles, who live there with their two daughters, Amy, aged 3, and Glenna, aged 5.
- The residents are reported to be safe, but one firefighter has been sent to hospital in an ambulance with a suspected broken foot.
- A large crowd has gathered, and thick smoke is still pouring from the fire.

Exercise 6.2

Write a well-crafted, 25-second news story from the following set of facts. You are writing for a late-evening newscast. A suggested version begins on page 228.

- Gay Pride Day was marked by a march through downtown today.
- Approximately 2000 participants joined in the noon-time march, which included 12 floats and two bands.
- Crowds estimated at 4000 to 5000 lined the parade route along Main Street and in Memorial Park, where the parade wound up.
- City council approved the parade permit two months ago in a controversial vote, won by only a two-vote margin, 11-9.
- There was one violent incident during the march when some onlookers shouted insults and obscenities and a scuffle broke out.
- Three people were arrested and charged with assault and resisting arrest.
- One was Councillor Howard Gleason, 44, of 55 Elm Street, who had led the fight against approval for today's parade.
- The other two arrested were Ronald Horton, 31, of 1991 Main Street, and Barry Tomkins, 28, of 646 Prairie Court.
- Gay and Lesbian Coalition spokesperson Gayle D'Angelo said "In spite of this minor incident, the event was a huge success in raising awareness of gays and lesbians in our city and in creating a sense of confidence and pride in the community."

7

Broadcast Style

We saw in Chapter 3 how writing for the eye — writing for print — differs substantially from writing for the ear — writing for broadcast. We've added the nuts and bolts of broadcast writing conventions and learned how to write that all-important first sentence, the lead. In this chapter, we'll look at broadcast writing as a stylistic expression. How do you choose your words and craft your sentences to develop your own writing style and to create the news sound that is most effective for radio and television?

Words

The words used in broadcast scripts must be chosen with great care. Although the result sometimes sounds casual or conversational on the air, this effect is not easily achieved. You've been trained in all the writing that you've done up to now to write at a formal level, that long, complicated words are better than short, simple ones. In writing that people will hear, we have to attempt to do just the opposite: to choose words that are short, clear, precise, and common. Unfortunately, not all broadcasters have received this message, so we often hear on radio or TV news pompous-sounding long words that supposedly add authority to the story. Try to get rid of such tendencies in your own writing. *Speak* to your audience.

COMMON AND CONVERSATIONAL WORDS

We hear phrases such as "The chief of police stated that the assailants fled on foot but were apprehended after a short chase." Is this the way you speak? If we are aiming at clear and common language, we certainly would never use "stated" for "said" or "assailants" for "attackers" or "robbers." And when was the last time you used "apprehended" when you were talking to your friends? Why not just "caught"?

The following list contains a few of the more common examples of non-conversational words that can be replaced with more common and simpler language.

Uncommon	Common/Conversational
acquire	get
altercation	argument
attorney	lawyer
commence	begin
conflagration/blaze	fire
deceased	dead
due to the fact that	because
end result	result
escalate	rise
in addition	besides
initiate	start
in the vicinity	near
intoxicated/inebriated	drunk
is of the opinion	believes
lacerations	cuts
male/female	man/woman
objective	aim/goal
physician	doctor
prior to	before
remuneration	pay
reside	live
residence	home
stated	said
terminate	end
this point in time	now
transpire	happen
utilize	use
vehicle	car
youth	teenager

Exercise 7.1

Revise the following sentences using simpler, easier to understand, common language better suited to broadcast. Suggested answers begin on page 229.

1. The decision to permit headgear to be worn on the premises of their establishment infuriated many members of the Legion.
2. A train derailment in the vicinity of Red Deer has resulted in a conflagration that is proving difficult to control.
3. The cost of employment insurance will escalate as of tomorrow due to the fact that there is currently a 600-billion-dollar shortfall in the fund.
4. Physicians at the local hospital are hoping to acquire new equipment that will have the end result of quicker diagnosis in some cancer cases.
5. Clorisco Industries will be terminating the employment of approximately 34 members of its workforce sometime in the near future.
6. The attorney for the convicted man is of the opinion that an appeal is a likelihood.
7. A witness who resides next door to the deceased victim stated that, prior to the accident, she heard an altercation between the man and an unknown male.
8. There are good tidings today for consumers who partake of the fare offered by the Downtown Shopping Centre. It is extending its hours of operation until 10 at night during the period of this month.
9. Law enforcement officers in our locality will be utilizing new weaponry after a decision by the police board last night to authorize usage of semi-automatic handguns.
10. The installation of two wheelchair ramps will bring the school into compliance with recently enacted provincial regulations requiring accessibility to all public structures.

OBJECTIVE WORDS

The words used in news stories must be simple, clear, precise, and common, but in selecting the words to use newswriters must remain objective. A listener will understand the following sentences differently.

Smith *claims* that he was at home at the time of the incident.

Smith *maintains* that he was at home at the time of the incident.

Smith *confirms* that he was at home at the time of the incident.

In the first sentence, Smith's whereabouts are in doubt. In the second, Smith has been accused of being elsewhere but denies it. In the third, it is assumed that Smith was at home, and he is merely agreeing with that assumption. One word makes a huge difference in how the listener understands what was said. Careless or thoughtless word choice can give listeners the wrong impression or just confuse them. Obviously, we must be careful to remain objective and not to make implications that are either in doubt or not true by using "loaded" words — those that carry value judgements. At worst, failure to observe this principle can result in a lawsuit (see Chapter 15).

There is a strong temptation sometimes to add colour to a story by inserting adjectives and adverbs. There is nothing wrong with making the story interesting, but your descriptions must not damage the objectivity of your report. Your opinion about the news must not be part of the script unless your report is clearly labelled an "editorial" or opinion piece.

The gunman luckily was arrested within hours.

Why "luckily"? Maybe the arrest was the result of excellent and thorough police work, but by adding the adverb we make it seem like a fluke.

Following her conviction, Gallant received only a six-month sentence.

Why "only"? Do we know better than the judge who tried the case? (In fact, here we are running dangerously close to contempt of court by criticizing the sentence handed down by the judge. See Chapter 15.)

Exercise 7.2

Underline the "loaded" words in each of the following sentences. Answers begin on page 229.

1. The price increase of only three dollars per ticket was announced today by the team owners.
2. A crowd of fewer than ten thousand showed up at Parliament Hill to protest the controversial proposal.
3. The fundraiser pulled in just three thousand dollars, but organizers said they were pleased.

4. Police in Manitoba have finally captured an escaped convict who has been on the loose since Wednesday.

5. The mayor insisted that the restructuring proposal will increase efficiency in the county clerk's office.

6. Developers estimate that about 200 new jobs will be created if their innovative plan is allowed to proceed.

7. Gerry Mason was attacked by a vicious dog as he innocently walked along Water Street at about 3:30 this morning.

8. The teenager was hit by a car as he staggered across MacLeod Road.

9. When the pretty 25-year-old was appointed to the position, she became the youngest city clerk in the 150-year history of the municipality.

10. The students fortunately called off their walkout when the administration threatened to take legal action.

JOURNALESE

Another area that deserves some attention in our discussion about choosing words is jargon and "journalese." Police and fire stories are particularly notorious for the use of trite old phrases, most of which are direct repetitions of police procedural jargon: "pending notification of next of kin," "dispatched to the scene," "guarded (or fair or stable) condition," "perpetrator," "arresting officer," "building was gutted," "innocent victim," "claimed the life," "war torn," "stiff opposition," and so on. Sports and weather are especially susceptible to the use of journalese; good reporters try to find new, better, more meaningful ways of expressing themselves than simply repeating the same old phrases: "netted a goal," "round-tripper," "come-from-behind victory," "ran up the score," "took one for the team," "dead last," "action-packed," and so on.

Exercise 7.3

Suggest easily understood alternatives to the following jargon and journalese. Suggested answers begin on page 230.

1. . . . pending notification of next of kin.
2. The perpetrator fled the scene on foot.
3. The building was gutted by the four-alarm blaze.
4. Police combed the neighbourhood for the missing toddler.
5. The highway death toll for the weekend.

CLICHÉS

Phrases that at one time were clever or appropriate or precise become clichés — trite and boring — through endless repetition. Like journalese, clichés should be avoided in your writing whenever possible — all your writing, not just your writing for broadcast. Find original, clear, simple ways of saying what you want without resorting to phrases such as "tried and true," "to the bitter end," "loud and clear," "toe the line," "stick to his guns," "crack of dawn," "the last straw," "at wits' end," "dog tired," and so on.

Exercise 7.4

Suggest more natural and simple alternatives to the clichés in the following sentences. Suggestions begin on page 230.

1. It remains to be seen if the tried-and-true methods are the best for this council.
2. When all is said and done, the torrid pace will take its toll on the early leaders.
3. Mayor Williams pulled no punches in telling council in no uncertain terms that he thought the proposal was out of the question.
4. The full extent of the damage has yet to be determined by police investigators.
5. At the crack of dawn, an artillery barrage broke the silence.

SPELLING AND WORD CONFUSION

You are writing for the ear, not the eye, so what does spelling matter? Why does the placement of an apostrophe make any difference? Who cares whether you write *accept* or *except* since they sound the same? The newsreader cares! To give a good, powerful read, the newscaster has to lift the words from the page and deliver them convincingly and confidently. This is not possible if the reader is confused about what the sentence means or where it is going. Ensure that the reader is comfortable with the material. It is the responsibility of a writer to check spelling carefully, especially the spelling of names and places (which your computer's spell checker can't help you with), to ensure that the reader can deliver them accurately.

How can an apostrophe change the meaning (and the reading) of a sentence?

The bailiff called the plaintiffs names.

The bailiff called the plaintiffs' names.

What does each sentence mean? If you are unsure about how to use an apostrophe, get a book on writing skills. The word *it's* is particularly troublesome. *It's* always means *it is* or *it has*; the possessive form is *its*.

Other words that can create havoc for a newsreader include look-alike words with meanings very different from each other. Using *affect* when you mean *effect* can so change the meaning of the sentence that a reader will be unable to deliver it properly. Using *lead* when you mean *led* causes the reader to mispronounce the word and makes the sentence completely meaningless. Other such troublesome words include *advice* and *advise*, *moral* and *morale*, *than* and *then*, *their* and *they're*, *whose* and *who's*, and *you're* and *your*. Learn how to use them correctly!

Exercise 7.5

As a test of your ability with sound-alike and look-alike words, try this exercise. If you get any of the words wrong, consider purchasing a good writing handbook as a reference or a writing skills text that will teach, test, and reinforce these and other important writing skills. Answers begin on page 230.

1. They're aren't many politicians who's private lives can stand up to the kind of examination sometimes conducted by the media.
2. It isn't you're fault that the client didn't chose are design for his stationary.
3. A nice Jaguar in a silver blue would be the perfect compliment for you're new jeans.
4. The council he gave you should led to piece of mind and higher moral.
5. She'd rather go were there is piece and quite then too a crowded mall.
6. If I take you're advise, I'll loose my personnel savings.
7. The effect of to much dinning out is that you have to loose weight.
8. How dose a person who's conscious bothers him ever do anything that conflicts with his principles?
9. Its latter then we thought, so we'll have to eat desert and leave.
10. A coarse in etiquette would teach you to avoid coarse language and to except compliments gracefully.

Sentences

Broadcast sentences, like the words, should be simple, clear, and conversational. Several formulas suggest how long a sentence should be. One says that a sentence over 20 words is too long. Another gets you to add up the number of syllables in your sentence and subtract the number of words. If the result is over 20, then your sentence needs shortening. In a newsroom, you don't have time to count words, let alone syllables, so simply remember what each method is trying to get you to do: keep your sentences short. An easier formula is that any sentence that exceeds three lines of normal print is too long in a news script. Of course, there is the danger of making all sentences so short that your script sounds choppy and abrupt, so try to have some variety in length. A newsreader can easily run two short sentences together to add flow to the sound of the newscast, but a sentence that is too long to get out in one breath can cause embarrassing problems for the reader.

ACTIVE

Sentences should contain "active" verbs, which involve action by the subject of the sentence; someone is *doing* something, not having something done to him or her.

Active: The man bought a new computer.

Passive: A new computer was bought by the man.

Active: More than 200 people donated blood.

Passive: Blood was donated by more than 200 people.

Active verbs are more interesting and dramatic than passive verbs, so they are used much more often in broadcast scripts. There's nothing wrong with passive verbs, but some writers have a tendency to overuse them and drain the story of all power and impact.

Exercise 7.6

Change all the following passive verbs to active verbs. Answers begin on page 230.

1. The ball was hit down the left-field line by Stevens and went into the crowd for a ground-rule double.
2. In France today, a demonstration was held by farmers who are afraid of losing their government subsidies.
3. A law has been passed by the provincial legislature that will force large corporations to pay a minimum tax.
4. The victory parade was observed by more than 40 thousand fans as it wound through downtown.
5. A man whose distant relative left him more than four million dollars has been located by private investigators.

GRAMMAR

Grammatical errors must be eliminated in all broadcast scripts. Again, it's a matter of credibility. Listeners who hear a newscaster using incorrect or just weak grammar immediately lose respect for the reader. They cannot trust the authority and credibility of someone who doesn't know how to speak correctly — and a newscaster who doesn't have the respect of the audience and whose credibility is suspect is out of business. Imagine that you are watching the nightly news and that the sharp-looking, serious, authoritative anchor is telling you about a fire: "Firefighters would of went into the building, but they didn't know nothing about the condition of the floor supports. Witnesses seen two people running from the building just before the fire begun." Would you have confidence in this person as your news authority?

There isn't space here to teach all the rules of correct grammar and expression, but you should learn some of the most common errors in broadcast scripts and how to avoid them. It is worth mentioning here that writing skills head the list of requirements for broadcast journalists according to surveys of news directors.

PRONOUN AGREEMENT

This grammatical rule has several aspects, some of them quite complex, but here we'll deal with two important points.

Tip 1. That *and* which *always refer to things;* who *and* whom *always refer to people.* Thus, "Everyone that attended the meeting . . ." is wrong; so is ". . . the candidate that was elected." This is one of the most common errors in broadcast writing. Remember that in your audience there are people who know this rule, and many others who know the sentence doesn't sound right even though they can't tell you which rule was broken. The result, once again, is loss of credibility.

Tip 2. *A pronoun must clearly refer to the correct antecedent.* The antecedent is the word that the pronoun replaces, so in the sentence "John thought that he was right" the pronoun, "he," replaces its antecedent, "John." In your writing, make sure that it is easy to understand which word is being replaced. Examples will make this mistake easier to understand and correct.

"Constable Jenkins introduced Raul Cortez to reporters and said that he had saved his life." Who saved whose life?

"The gunman hit the cash register with his gun, breaking it." What was broken?

Listeners have a hard enough time understanding everything on one hearing so don't force them to decipher unclear sentences such as these.

Exercise 7.7

Correct the pronoun problems in these sentences. Answers begin on page 230.

1. Police are requesting anyone that might have seen something that evening to call the emergency hotline.
2. The number of people that are out of work has fallen for the third consecutive month.
3. Parade organizers gave a large trophy to the best float, which they had found in the basement of City Hall.
4. Sommers told Gionelli that he had beaten him fairly.
5. The committee accused city council of failing to account for its expenditures when it presented its financial statement.

MISPLACED MODIFIERS

Place descriptive words as close as possible to the words that they describe. Doing so is particularly critical with the words *only*, *almost*, *just*, and *nearly* but applies to all modifiers. The problem is one of meaning and can lead to serious mistakes.

The witness told the judge only what she had heard. (nothing else)

The witness told only the judge what she had heard. (no one else)

The witness told the judge what she had only heard. (not seen)

The witness only told the judge what she had heard. (didn't do anything else)

Each of these sentences means something different. Precise placement of limiting words such as those mentioned above requires a moment of thought. Take the time to ensure that your meaning is clear to a listener. Other types of misplaced modifiers cause humour more than confusion.

Opposition members called on the minister of defence to resign during a news conference.

While on patrol, the officers discovered a man who had been shot to death in their cruiser.

Exercise 7.8

Rewrite these sentences to correct the placement of modifiers and clarify the meaning of the sentence. Answers begin on page 231.

1. Handcuffed together and wearing leg irons, police officers brought the accused men into the heavily guarded courtroom.
2. The United Way almost collected 30 thousand dollars in the first week of the spring fundraising campaign.
3. Taxes will nearly rise seven percent next year.
4. The driver was rescued by an emergency crew after swerving off the road and becoming trapped in the wrecked car.
5. After almost getting a sentence of 30 years in jail, the judge also fined the convicted man ten thousand dollars.

SUBJECT-VERB AGREEMENT

A verb and its subject must "agree" in number. In other words, if the subject of a sentence is *singular* (referring to one thing or person), then the verb must also be singular. If the subject is plural (referring to more than one thing or person), then the verb must be plural.

> The judge [singular subject] who gave first prize to these entries was [singular verb] too generous. (A common error would be to make the verb plural — "were" — to agree with "entries," which is not the subject of the sentence.)

> Four pages [plural subject] of information were [plural verb] released to the media.

Exercise 7.9

Rewrite these sentences to correct the errors in subject–verb agreement. Answers begin on page 231.

1. Cloud-seeding to enhance rainfall and prevent snowstorms were expected to be a breakthrough in weather control.
2. The bizarre lives of many rock stars captivates the attention of young fans.

3. Everybody we see at the wrestling matches cheer for The Mad Austrian.
4. Many cities in Russia has a "kremlin" because the word simply signify a fortress or citadel.
5. The rate of business bankruptcies are rising monthly.
6. All of us at the college thinks that cheating and plagiarism is a serious offence.
7. The variety of Richard's money-making activities are amazing: Richard plays cards, bets on horses, and sells stocks.
8. One can't help noticing that the members of the orchestra is playing better now that the conductor is sober.
9. At lunchtime, our cafeteria, with its dreary salad bar, greasy chips, and soggy burgers, take away my appetite.
10. The reason for Canada's success in the downhill races were many years of hard work by our skiers.

Assignments

1. Clip three stories from a newspaper and highlight any words or passages that do not meet the standards of broadcast style. Watch especially for uncommon words, journalese, and passive verbs.
2. Do the same with an essay or report that you wrote recently. Would converting it to broadcast style improve the writing or just make it different?
3. Write a short story that deliberately violates as many of the points in this chapter as possible. Exchange stories with a colleague for correction.

Unit Two
Review Exercises

Rewrite the following sentences to make them conform to correct broadcast style. These are not lead sentences. No answers are provided for these review exercises.

1. In court, Constable Salfi said that he told the accused that his partner was behind him. Under cross-examination, the officer sadly revealed that he had been lying.
2. Only 9% of the 1,200 respondents to the poll agreed that the environment was the biggest issue in the election. More than 52.3% said that unemployment was the most important concern in this region.
3. Pleasing people is Pam Prudhomme's primary purpose in life. The new owner of Hilltop Resort Hotel, Pam was officially welcomed to the community this morning at 9 a.m. in a ceremony hosted by the mayor.
4. Sunday, sunshine should send some warmer weather our way. The forecast for the early part of the week also looks good.
5. The accused, William James, appeared in court for a bail hearing this morning. Mr. James is charged with assault.
6. The parks and recreation office in this city is a complete joke. This is the opinion of Ms. Gail Kozelski, who is trying to get permission to use a city-owned baseball diamond for her semi-pro baseball team.
7. Two people were killed in a single-car collision this morning at the corner of Capstone and South Sts. on the east side of the city, and according to police reports, traffic in the area remains blocked, with rush-hour traffic backing up several kilometres right onto the expressway, which has caused difficulty for ambulance and police vehicles trying to get to the scene.
8. Councillor Syndi Toorbie said, "This is the worst decision from the mayor's office that I have seen since I came on council 8 years ago." She and Gareth Baker were the only councillors apposed to the proposed by-law.
9. The Blues and the Falcons fought to a 2-2 tie tonight in a regional junior hockey match-up. It was a wild-and-woolly affair, with neither side giving an inch but going toe to toe until the final bell.
10. Thieves escaped with $4,529 from a downtown restaurant today at 11 a.m. Police later arrested Mr. Kevin Mettle of 56 Acorn Dr. and charged him with robbery and possession of stolen property.

Review 2.2

Correct or improve the following leads.

1. A robbery happened at 3 a.m. at the gas station on Mason Avenue. Two armed men threatened the attendant and got away with 200 dollars. . . .
2. A pet cat woke the James family last night in time to allow them to escape from their burning home, which had caught fire as the result of faulty wiring in an electric heater and took firefighters more than three hours to bring under control. The cat, named Buster, is being given the credit. . . .
3. Mrs. Debbie Kreuz of Parkside Court in Riverbend has been charged with sexual assault in a case involving her daughter's babysitter. Police brought charges after complaints from. . . .
4. There was an accident last night. Three local teens were injured. . . .
5. Why did James Fitch of Queen Street beat his wife with a bottle? The judge who convicted him yesterday said there was evidence that. . . .

Review 2.3

Using the following information, write stories for use at a local station. Don't forget to spend extra time composing that all-important lead sentence and to correct any errors in broadcast style in the sentences.

1. • Teachers at Vincent Massey High School rejected a contract offer from the school board at a meeting in the school auditorium last night.
   • The vote was 146 to 71 against the two-year offer, which would have given them a 4% raise in the first year and 3% in the second year.
   • The president of the teachers' union, Ms. Ida Levine, said, "The money was fine, but the issue is class size, not cash." The teachers want a cap on the number of students in each class.
   • The current contract expires this week, and the teachers may strike legally at the beginning of next month, but a strike vote has not yet been taken.

2. • Sandy Pleasance, 15, of 731 Maple St., won the Canadian national junior chess championship.
   • She was competing in the championship held in Saint. John, N.B., all last week. Last night she defeated Kevin Wong, 14, from Toronto to claim the top spot.
   • Pleasance is a grade 10 student at Vincent Massey High School, where she is also president of the chess club and an honours student.
   • She has been playing chess since she was 5 and has been city junior champion for the past 2 years, and she even finished 3rd in the senior

championship last year. This was her first time in competition at the national level.
- In the championship, she won 5 games and drew 2, just beating Wong, who won 5, lost 1, and drew 1.

3. • Douglas Thibeault (TEE-bo), 37, of 456 King St., was shot in the shoulder at 4 a.m. while sitting in the Donut Express on Harvest Blvd.
- Witnesses said that a woman came into the store with him and that they began to argue. They say that two shots were fired.
- Mr. Thibeault's wife, Janet, 34, was arrested by Constable Elizabeth Cinelli (chin-EL-ee) at the scene. Mrs. Thibeault is an employee of Brookes Fabricating Ltd. and is of Hungarian ancestry. Her husband is French-Canadian and works at Tallman Realty Ltd.
- Mr. Thibeault is in good condition at City Hospital with a bullet wound in the shoulder. Police say a .38-calibre handgun was seized. No charges have been laid yet, and the investigation continues.

Note: As you will learn when we cover journalism and the law, you may not convict Mrs. Thibeault until a judge has done so. In other words, you may not say she shot her husband. You may say she has been arrested, but you may not say anything that would directly connect her with the person who shot Mr. Thibeault. She might, in fact, be innocent.

Review 2.4

Rewrite the following stories to make them acceptable for broadcast. All of the guidelines in this unit are needed to correct these passages fully.

1. The prime minister was met by a group of rude and unreasonable protesters when he arrived at Halifax Airport this afternoon. The group objected to the government's proposal to force people off welfare and unemployment funding and into training and upgrading programs that would make them more employable in the future, but a spokesperson for the protesters, Lilian Smythe, said, "If were in classes we can't be out looking for jobs, so their just making a bad situation worse." The prime minister tried to address the crowd, but they wouldn't except his arguments and shouted him down. He is in Halifax for a meeting of first ministers from across the country.

2. A famous Canadian died. Stan Pender was best known as a researcher who lead the medical team that made several important discoveries about the cause of cystic fibrosis. Stan won many awards for his research and was nominated for the Nobel prize in medicine. His discoveries helped to pinpoint the cause of cystic fibrosis. This may one

day lead to a cure for the disease. Stan died in Montreal last night at the age of 61 from AIDS-related causes. By finding the cause of cystic fibrosis, his research helped thousands of victims of the disease to live longer and more normal lives with improved drugs and treatment. Stan was 61.

3. There was a debate at last night's city council meeting. In a nutshell, the problem was a proposed rezoning to permit an after-hours club to operate in the west-side residential neighbourhood of Mountainside. The spokesperson for the developers, Patricia Dunlop, said, "It will provide a place for young people to go instead of getting into trouble, and it will mean up to twenty jobs for staff." On the other side of the coin, the residence were represented by Mr. Clare Hastings, 48, of Hastings and Dove law firm. He said, "The traffic, noise, and rowdiness will disturb residents until after 4 a.m., reduce property values, and breed crime." Council split evenly on the rezoning application, with the mayor casting the deciding vote. It was basically a tempest in a teapot, but when all was said and done it had got residents up in arms. Maybe they'll vote differently in next month's municipal elections now that they have saw council in action.

Assignment

Broadcast journalism, unlike many professions, allows a learner to see and hear professionals doing their jobs all the time, to learn from them, to evaluate their performances. There isn't a more valuable activity for a prospective broadcast writer, reporter, or newscaster who wishes to learn the craft than to study the people on the air. Make a habit of monitoring newscasts every day, and keep a log like the one below. Listen to a variety of stations and newscasters, and tune in at different times of the day to get a broad perspective on the news profession in your area.

Date	Station	Time	Length	Newscaster
_____	_____	_____	_____	_____

Top story

_____

No. of stories

_____

No. of local stories

_____

Comments and impressions

_____

UNIT 3

Gathering the News

8

Interviewing

Much of what a reporter does is listen to people in order to get the information that goes into the news story. The people might be police officers, robbery victims, politicians, hockey players, firefighters, union leaders, or witnesses of an event. They might be very used to talking with reporters or terrified of doing so. They might have pat answers well rehearsed, or they might be almost speechless. The reporter's job is first to get the information that the public will want to know, second to get a usable recording of the person, and third to investigate promising lines of questioning that might lead to previously unrevealed information of value. Good reporters are good interviewers. While some are naturally more comfortable than others in conducting interviews, anyone who aspires to be a good professional reporter should develop techniques and skills that will make interviews more productive.

The Golden Rule

There is an easy-to-remember, one-word rule that will make you a better interviewer: *listen*. The biggest fault among ineffective interviewers, beginner and veteran alike, is their inability to follow this rule. Many are nervous about the interview, especially if the subject is someone who is famous or has a position of authority, so they develop a list of questions that they ask one after the other without paying much attention to the responses; when they hear a pause, they figure the question has been answered and go on to the next one. This question-and-answer technique will inevitably result in missing an important story or in asking a question that has already been answered.

In interviewing the president of a company charged with pollution, a reporter asked, "Has your firm ever been accused of these activities in the past?" and got the reply "We have a very good environmental record. The other charges were thrown out of court." The reporter heard a pause and asked the next question on her list, missing a potentially important line of questioning. Many times, reporters who don't listen to the answers will ask a question only to be told by the subject "I just answered that." People being interviewed will often expand on an answer or even anticipate the next question.

The best interviews are conversations. Certainly, a reporter must have an idea of what the interview ought to be about and should have questions planned (see "Preparation" below), but after the first question it is best to let the interview take a conversational tone and fall back on the prepared questions only when the conversation stops. Follow-up questions such as "Why do you say that?" or "Could you explain what you mean by that?" or "How will you accomplish that?" are very effective in getting to the meat of an issue. They are better than a fencing match in which you try to get good answers to your prepared questions, and the interviewee waits for the question that will allow him or her to present the important information.

Preparation

Unfortunately, adequate preparation for an interview is a luxury afforded only to weekly public affairs and news magazine shows. Such programs have a staff of researchers and assistants and several weeks in which to prepare for each story. The on-the-job radio or TV reporter, however, may cover several stories in a day, and those stories may be as diverse as an interview with a little-league hockey coach who has quit to protest against the violence in his league, a session with the minister of agriculture, who is visiting the city on a speaking tour, and an interview with the city councillor who is fighting the Public Works Department's budget proposal. Not only does the reporter not have enough time to research the issues involved thoroughly, but also she probably won't have the expertise on all these subjects (or the incredibly wide range of subject matter she'll have to cover tomorrow and the next day as well) to be able to ask clever or revealing questions. The best she can do is ask the questions she thinks the audience might want to have answered. This is another reason, of course, that a journalist must be an information junkie, accumulating background information all the time.

Whatever preparation time is available must be spent productively. Read everything you can about the issue in the newspapers, supplied news release, court documents, minutes of meetings, even an encyclopedia or reference book. Talk to everyone who will talk to you: other reporters, people affected by the issue, opponents, supporters. Get a feel for the story. Where is the conflict? What are the issues? Who are the players? Why has this happened? Take the time to write down the three or four (no more) questions that must be answered in the course of the interview. Perhaps you won't have to refer to them during the interview, but having written them down will help you to focus on the direction you expect the conversation to take. You should go into the interview with a clear sense of where the conversation is likely to go but with the confidence to let it go in other directions as well. Check your list if the conversation reaches a dead end and when the interview is nearing the end to make sure you've covered everything.

Another vital part of your preparation is to ensure that your equipment is working properly. Check all batteries before leaving the station, and carry replacement batteries. Test the recorder and the tape, and take spare tape. Test the microphone and all the connections, and take extra cable and connectors. Check the levels on location, and do a test and playback before beginning the interview. (See Chapters 21 and 22 for the special attention TV reporters must take to ensure a properly recorded interview.) These measures cannot be emphasized enough. The horror stories from inexperienced (and even veteran) reporters who lost the interview of a lifetime or were thoroughly humiliated because of faulty or missing equipment would fill several books.

Exercise 8.1

Prepare a list of the three or four "must ask" questions that you might use to interview the people in the following scenarios. Of course, without access to more research, you will have to go on what information you have and use your judgement and imagination to come up with questions that should produce useful responses. Share your answers with others to develop skill in thinking of significant questions.

1. You will interview the witness of an airplane crash. Karen Dykstra is an amateur pilot and was checking over her plane before a flight today when the four-seat aircraft was coming in for a landing. It hit the runway nose-first, flipped over, and caught on fire. Both people inside were killed instantly. They have not been identified; the plane was from another city.

2. You will interview a city councillor about his objections to a walking trail that has been proposed. The trail will begin at a shopping centre, wind for six kilometres through a residential neighbourhood, and end at a park. Those in favour of the trail say it will be a shortcut for resi-

dents, provide recreational activity for walkers, cyclists, and skiers in the winter, and help to erase traffic congestion on roads around the shopping centre. Councillor Perelli, however, spoke up at last night's council meeting to say it would be a waste of money and would become a dangerous attraction for muggers and others who want to engage in illegal or immoral activity.

3. You will interview the director of the local humane society. The animal shelter run by the society is 30 years old and has been criticized many times as being crowded, dirty, and outdated. The director, Tessa Jorgenssen, has issued a news release saying that the society is going to launch a fundraising campaign to get enough money (120 thousand dollars is the amount in the release) to build a new shelter. She hopes that the city and the province will donate matching amounts, which will be enough to pay for construction.

The Subject

There are several schools of thought on how to treat an interview subject or "interviewee." Some reporters think that their job is to be antagonistic, to bully the subject into "coming clean." This approach may work for Geraldo because, to be successful, he must be a part of the story; if a subject walks out or takes a swing at him, that's better entertainment for his viewers than a thoughtful and complete response. For most reporters and most situations, a polite, considerate, and conversational interview will produce the best results. The vast majority of interviews that a reporter will file will not be confrontational, with the subject in the hot seat; most will be informational, with the subject in the position of supplying detail, an eyewitness account, insight, or specialized information. In such situations, it is important to make the interviewee feel relaxed and unthreatened.

 Tip 1. *Make your equipment as unobtrusive as possible.* A camera or a microphone can be dreadfully intimidating to those who are not used to performing in front of them. Work with the camera person to keep the camera as far as possible from the subject and, if possible, out of his or her direct line of vision. Use the smallest microphone that will give you effective results, and hold it down, away from the person's face. If possible, use a lapel microphone. Some of the most effective interviews with difficult sub-

jects have been achieved by using only the built-in microphone on the tape recorder, starting the machine, and leaving it lying unobtrusively on the table between the interviewer and the subject. Unfortunately, this method does not give the high-quality broadcast sound that technicians like, but it has produced some of the most revealing and most moving interviews.

Tip 2. *Warm up the subject before getting to the questions.* In fact, it is best not to break from the warm-up before beginning the interview. With the tape running, talk about the weather, about the Flames or the Blue Bombers or the Jays, about the previous story you covered, and then move the subject around to the matter at hand. If you begin with the toughest question, the subject may become defensive or frightened and may not provide full or natural answers.

Tip 3. *Try to use the conversational tone all the way through the session, even though the questions might be tough or critical.* One way of deflecting the antagonism that might result from a critical question is to say, "Your critics are saying . . ." or "People seem to want to know why . . ." or "In the paper today, they say. . . ." However, do not apologize for questions or abandon your neutrality. The reporter must be objective and give no clue about her or his personal point of view; it is unfair to the interviewee and to the audience to do otherwise.

Tip 4. *Maintain eye contact with the subject, and give your undivided attention to what is said.* Doing so is not only courteous but also helps to maintain the conversational atmosphere that will produce the best results from the interview. TV reporters who keep glancing at the camera operators or checking their watches while the subject speaks are both impolite and ineffective; the interviewee is not likely to provide such people with anything more than basic information and the shortest answers possible. Why talk when you're not being listened to? Reporters have been seen to turn off the tape recorder or walk away with the microphone while the subject is still speaking. Their attitude is "We got what we came for, let's get back to the station." Such bad manners have helped to give reporters the reputation of boorish, aggressive, single-minded vultures that is so widespread and makes it more and more difficult to get co-operation from the public.

Tip 5. *Keep quiet.* Do not encourage your subject by answering "Yes" or making sympathetic and encouraging "Uh-huh" sounds at the end of each answer or during a pause. Such interruptions create problems in the editing room when you're trying to get a clean sound bite of the person's statement.

Questions

 Tip 1. *Avoid questions with one-word answers.* "Yes" does not make a very interesting or useful taped insert for your story. Questions must be phrased to elicit full responses, ideally in the 15-to-30-second range. While you have no control over the length of the answer (except in the editing room), you can avoid asking questions that produce "Yes" or "No" answers. "Does this mean there will be a strike?" is likely to produce "Yes" for an answer. How might the question be better phrased? Under the pressure of the interview, you might ask a question that gets a one-word response, but a follow-up question asking for clarification or reasons can rescue the situation and get you a usable clip.

 Tip 2. *Avoid "leading" questions.* These are questions that suggest answers: "You must have been angry when the suspect was released?" This type of question clearly fishes for controversy by putting ideas, if not words, into the mouth of the subject. It is unfortunately common in even the most professional interview. Frustrated with a calm or careful subject, reporters sometimes resort to asking leading questions in the hope of getting a more dramatic clip to use. This approach does not serve the audience or the interviewee well and often leads to one-word answers anyway. Instead of the question above, a more neutral question would be "How do you feel about the release of John Doe?" Reporters have been known to take leading questions to extremes: "This refusal by the government to listen to your group will force you to use violence, right?" This question is clearly unprofessional and unethical.

 Tip 3. *Re-ask a question.* A good technique that often produces unexpected and interesting results is to rephrase a question: ask the same question again but in different words. When a subject answers in generalities or avoids a direct answer, an alert reporter will either re-ask the question right away or wait for a few minutes and then re-ask it. Sometimes an interviewee will be caught off guard by the rephrased question and answer it more fully or even contradict the first answer.

 Tip 4. *Wait for a response.* Another technique that is very productive is to use silence. On-air people are taught that "dead air" is the worst thing that can happen, but for a reporter conducting an interview it can be very worthwhile. A subject will almost always be compelled to add something or expand on the answer if the reporter continues to hold the microphone and wait while maintaining eye contact.

Problem Subjects

RELUCTANCE

The subject who does not want to appear on camera or on tape is more common than you might think. Because they have been burnt by past contacts with the media, or because they are naturally shy or afraid, or just because they don't like their own looks or voices, people routinely refuse to be interviewed. Some resist all efforts at persuasion, but here are a few suggestions that have worked with such people.

Tell the reluctant subject how important it is that his or her side of the story be made public. If listeners and viewers get only the opposition's point of view, then they will never know that another opinion has validity.

Reassure nervous subjects that you will redo the interview if they freeze or break up or go blank. This technique should be used judiciously, though, because you do not want to give a subject right of approval to your story before it goes on the air. However, telling subjects that a retake is possible is fine, as long as you do not suggest they can decide what you may use and what you may not use.

Get them talking. If they will talk without the recorder rolling, then you can point out that they've just done a rehearsal, so it will be easy to do it again with the tape recording. Some reporters have suggested doing a rehearsal and then rolling the tape; at the end of the "rehearsal," they reassure the subject that it was a great interview and ask for permission to use it.

LONG-WINDEDNESS

Some subjects talk until your tape runs out. Of course, most of what they say will be unusable, so to get the clip you need it is necessary to interrupt them. The best way to do this is to wait until the subject hits a point that is important, interrupt as politely as possible, and then mention that what she or he has just said is of real interest to your audience. Would it be possible to have it repeated? The second time through, the subject will likely be more concise. Another possibility is to let the subject wind down and then ask specific questions or take all the tape back to the station and edit to select the clips that you can use.

OFF-THE-RECORD AND ANONYMOUS INTERVIEWS

There is no legal obligation not to use material that you are told is "off the record." However, there are compelling moral and practical reasons not to use it. If you "burn" a source by using information that you said would be confidential, then you will never be able to use that source again. Chances are, if that person is a politician or public figure, that you will also be unable to get any information from the associates, party members, friends, or co-workers of the subject you betrayed. Treat off-the-record information as a beginning point for research or as material for questioning others.

Anonymous sources who give you information they want you to use, but who don't want their names in the news, are dangerous. Never use their information without substantiating it independently. If you can be sure from other sources that it is true, then you may use it with caution. However, if the information turns out to be evidence in court, then be prepared to reveal your source or be charged with contempt of court (see Chapter 15). Before considering the use of such information, ask yourself why it has been given to you; obviously, you are being used by someone, but why?

Exercise 8.2

This role-playing exercise involves teams of two people. One person assumes one of the roles listed below, is given five minutes to jot down detail and background that will flesh out the role, and is then interviewed by the second member of the team. The interviewer, meanwhile, should use the time to prepare questions. After the interview, the roles are reversed: the interviewee becomes the interviewer, and the interviewer assumes a role (a different role from the first one). When both interviews are complete, the interviewers will use their notes or tapes of the interviews to write a report for broadcast. Each interviewee should check the report for accuracy and suggest lines of questioning that would have been productive.

Roles

- a Canadian astronaut about to go into space aboard the space shuttle to do experiments on motion sickness in a weightless environment
- a member of the Olympic swimming (hockey/diving/skiing/gymnastic . . .) team in training for the next Olympic games
- a person who has just been awarded the Firefighters' Medal for Bravery for diving into an icy pond to save a drowning seven-year-old girl
- a broadcast journalist who has just won the Gemini Award as best TV reporter

Assignments

1. Record a news interview on radio or television. Evaluate the interviewer's performance under the following headings.

    a. knowledge of subject and apparent interest in the subject

    b. value and level of the questions (did you find out what you wanted to know?)

    c. follow-up questions

    d. conversational flow of the interview

    e. overall impressions

2. Schedule an interview with a teacher or other professional whose work interests you. Research the subject of the interview in advance, prepare questions, and conduct and record the interview. From this material, write three news stories.

Reporting Basics

In this chapter, we'll look at the normal day-to-day diet of the local news-cast; later we'll survey some of the specialty coverage such as sports, entertainment, and business. While the wire services keep us informed about the national and international events that have news value, reporters, news-readers, and newswriters recognize that local news is most often made up of meetings (political and otherwise), crimes, and accidents. There are no shortcuts to good coverage of these "bread and butter" news events, but there are some techniques and ideas that will make your coverage more effective.

Fire

Most stations have a police monitor in the newsroom that is tuned in to the police and fire dispatchers' bands. This radio alerts the newsroom when police or firefighters are responding to a call and can assist a news director in knowing how and when to assign reporters. This radio by itself must not be used as a source of broadcast stories; often the most dire emergency broadcast by the dispatcher will turn out to be a false alarm or a complete-ly different situation from that first reported.

Whether a particular fire will be covered or not is largely dependent on the severity of the disaster and the size of the broadcast market. If every Toronto or Montreal station broadcast every fire in the city, there would be little time for other news, so only those fires that have huge property loss-es, fatalities, and/or major disruption to traffic will make the newscast. On the other hand, in a small market every fire siren can become neighbour-hood news, so a fire need not be so large on the disaster scale for it to receive major coverage.

Naturally, a reporter on location is the best coverage. But aside from the obvious pictures or descriptions of the scene, there are many other angles that an alert reporter will consider. An interview with the fire official in charge is mandatory but not always easy; the fire officer's job is to put out the fire, not talk to reporters. A request for a short interview when the officer has a free minute is more likely to succeed than a more abrupt approach. It is important to find out if there are any fatalities or injuries, what caused the fire and how it was discovered, what the damage estimate is, where the owner of the building is, and whether any unusual problems are being encountered in putting the fire out. The fire official might not know the answers to these questions yet, but they have to be asked and re-asked until they're answered.

In the case of a private residence that is burning, a reporter will have to decide how intrusive to be. Is it all right to put a microphone in the face of a man who is watching his home burn to the ground? If members of his family are trapped inside? Some reporters would say that this is their job, that their audience would want them to do this regardless of how difficult it may be, that they are performing a public service in demonstrating the human side of such a tragedy. Others would say that the man has a right to privacy and that an audience would be offended by such an intrusion into private grief. We will return to these difficult decisions in our discussion of privacy in the chapter on journalistic ethics.

A commercial or industrial fire may not have the same potential for immediate personal tragedy, but an alert reporter will check whether the building was insured, how many people will be put out of work and for how long, and what was manufactured or stored in the building.

Crime

It is very uncommon for a reporter to be on the scene of a crime in progress, so almost all crime news is reported after the fact on information received from the police investigating the incident. Normally, the dispatcher (or usual police contact) will provide basic information, but it is often valuable to speak to the officer in charge of the investigation. The dispatcher is a busy person and is not always willing to spend time talking with a reporter, but this person is a vital link to a major source of your news and well worth cultivating. Many reporters have found that a curt "Anything going on?" will get an equally curt "No. Goodbye." Yet when they ask "Have any traffic accidents been reported this afternoon?" or "Have there been any arrests in your division this evening?" they will get information. Reporters who are polite, friendly, and make themselves known to the dispatcher are also much more likely to get information than those who treat the dispatcher as a nuisance.

Many police forces have a media relations officer who can be contacted when you need more information. This is still a new field for most forces, and sometimes the media relations people see their job as protecting the officers from unfavourable publicity rather than making information available. More and more, however, the police are trying to improve their relations with the media, and a smart reporter will try to win the trust of the media relations personnel. Generally, police officers, like anyone else, will respect fair, complete coverage and will be angered by unfair, incomplete, or uninformed reporting — whether favourable or critical.

While the street-wise reporter who digs his or her way through the clues and beats the police to the criminal is completely a work of fiction, reporters do not need to be entirely dependent on the police for all of their information. Robbery victims, witnesses, and neighbours have been interviewed in crime coverage. When a convenience store was held up, one enterprising reporter interviewed a panel of six convenience store employees, owners, and customers from the same part of town to get their views on the extent of the problem.

When reporting an arrest, it is vital that you do not convict the suspect in your coverage. To say that the accused person *committed* the crime is to risk a charge of contempt of court (see Chapter 15). Until a judge has pronounced the person guilty, that person is innocent. Therefore, you may say that John Doe has been arrested for armed robbery, that he is accused of holding up a bank, and that police say he had a gun on him — but you may not say that John Doe held up a bank with a gun. When writing these kinds of stories, keep in mind that the person may be acquitted; how can you phrase your coverage so that if that should happen no one can say your story was wrong?

Furthermore, many news organizations discourage the mention of an arrested person's name until charges have been laid. In big stories, this consideration is often waived, but the story must clearly indicate that the person has been arrested for questioning and has not been charged with a crime. In the same vein, be cautious about using everything a police official tells you. Quoting such an official doesn't mean that you are immune from a libel charge. When speaking to the media, many police officers are not careful in their phrasing and may state clearly who caused an accident or who fired a shot long before any charges are laid. If you quote them, you can be charged with libel or contempt of court. Finally, simply using the word *alleged* is not sufficient to save you from such charges. Wording must be much less incriminating than what is achieved by tossing an "alleged" here and there into the script.

Exercise 9.1

Examine each of the following lines from newscasts and determine which convict a person wrongly and which are okay for broadcast. Then rewrite those that are wrong. Answers begin on page 231.

1. A light truck, driven by Jane Sutherland of Centre Street, hit Harriet Trevain as she was crossing the street. Sutherland has been charged with careless driving.
2. After the burglar alarm went off, a man ran across Highway 61 and was struck by a car. Filmon Wright is under guard in hospital with a broken leg.
3. Two shots were fired during the scuffle. Terry Verveen of Calgary was arrested and charged with attempted murder and several weapons offences.
4. Following the accident, Renatta Scarlatti was charged by police because she was legally drunk and her licence was under suspension.
5. According to witnesses, William Perrin entered the store and pointed a gun at the cashier. When he had all the money, Perrin ran from the store and jumped into a black car driven by another man.

Accidents

As with crimes, most information about accidents comes from the police after the fact. If the accident is significant in your judgement, and deserves more than brief coverage, you can ask the dispatcher to give you the name of the investigating officer and contact that person to get details. Of course, some officers will be more forthcoming than others and some more available to the media than others. Reporters who establish a good rapport with police officers will always get better information than those whom the officers don't know or don't like. Follow-up information can be obtained from hospitals, firefighters (if they were called in for a fire or to remove an occupant from a vehicle), tow truck operators, witnesses, and friends or family members of victims.

Local Government

Politicians and reporters have a strange, symbiotic, but mutually distrustful relationship: politicians supply reporters with information that often makes good stories, and reporters supply politicians with air time — publicity. But each thinks of the other as an opponent. Politicians at the provincial and national levels, and to a lesser degree at the municipal level, are given instruction in media relations. They are taught how to get access to the media, how to speak in quotable-length clips, and how to handle difficult questions. Reporters and newswriters have to decide when they are being given a legitimate story and when (or to what extent) they are being used. Access to politicians is usually not difficult for reporters, but most public officials want to know in advance the subject of the interview so they can prepare themselves.

Covering city and town council meetings is a job that virtually every station must do, and it's often not the favourite assignment for reporters. Such meetings can go on for hours and raise so many issues (most of them simply not newsworthy) that attending them hardly seems to be worth all the time and effort. However, because local politics affects your audience so directly, it is essential that such meetings are well covered. Usually, the same reporter will handle municipal politics as a beat assignment, because the issues must really be followed week after week to get an understanding of what is important, who the players are, and when a good story is developing. Even veterans, however, must prepare themselves by reading the agendas and reports that are routinely sent to each radio and TV station and newspaper. Armed with this preview material, a good reporter can even begin to package the story before attending the meeting, getting interviews about the issues, and talking to the politicians or citizens who are most concerned with the newsworthy items.

Some reporters will tape the whole meeting and then go back to the station to edit it all down into usable clips. Others will go on their instincts, turning on the camera (if one is allowed in the chambers) or tape recorder when their preparation or reporter's sixth sense tells them a useful item is coming up. Generally, the best material is gained after the meeting or during breaks when the participants, whether politicians or involved citizens, are accessible to the media in the hallway outside the meeting or sometimes in a special media room.

A three- or four-hour municipal council meeting might have five or six newsworthy items, and it takes a knowledgeable and well-prepared reporter to produce stories that present them fairly, accurately, and interestingly. It is important to remember, though, that such coverage is your station's bread and butter, and you will be expected to produce three or four radio stories with taped inserts (at least one complete TV package) from any meeting you cover. It is for information on matters such as local tax rates, school board decisions, zoning changes, or parking by-laws — issues that directly affect your audience — that people tune in to you and not to distant stations whose news is not local.

Boards of education, commissions, committee meetings, important club meetings (Chamber of Commerce, etc.), and all manner of official gatherings are covered by thorough local news-oriented stations and their reporters. As with council meetings, the best stories will be filed by reporters who are familiar with the background and the current material. Usually, the best tape is acquired during breaks in the proceedings, when the principals can be interviewed and asked to summarize or recap their statements.

Courts

One of the principles of the Canadian judicial system is that court proceedings should be public; in the words of an old adage, "Justice must not only be done but also be seen to be done." For this reason, it is one of the media's responsibilities to cover the courts, which often provide important stories that attract and fascinate an audience. Sometimes, for specific and compelling reasons, a judge may exclude the public from a courtroom or forbid publication of parts or all of what goes on during a trial. Usually, this is done to protect innocent people (e.g., the victims in a sexual assault trial) or to ensure that someone else involved in the crime will get a fair trial. By and large, however, the courts are open to reporters.

News organizations generally cover only the most important and sensational courtroom procedures since our courts operate virtually non-stop during every working day; no one could (or would want to) cover everything. Even trials deemed worth covering sometimes go on for many days, even weeks. Often reporters are thrust into a trial at the beginning to report on the charges, the pleas, the atmosphere in the courtroom, et cetera, and then return at the end to hear the verdict. Few electronic news organizations have full-time court reporters. This means that a reporter assigned to cover a court story can be easily confused and intimidated by the unfamiliar and bewildering proceedings that are often shockingly unlike TV courtroom dramas. Preparation is the key for covering the courts. Read everything you can about the trial and what led up to it. Get all the paperwork that the court will provide, including the indictment (the formal charges laid against an accused person), read it, and get help to understand it if necessary. Most important, try to attend court proceedings once in a while. Become familiar with what goes on, what is permitted, and who the players are. Then, when you are assigned courtroom coverage, you will at least be familiar with the physical surroundings and the basic procedures.

One other piece of advice: get and read *A Reporter's Guide to Canada's Criminal Justice System* by Harold J. Levy, published by the Canadian Bar Association. This is a well-written, clear, and easy-to-understand guide, written specifically for reporters by a reporter and editor. It is part of an invaluable series of five little books called *Law and the Media*, and we'll refer to them again in Chapter 15.

In writing about court proceedings, whether you have actually covered the trial or not, it's necessary to be familiar with the terminology. Here are some of the most common terms you'll run across.

allegation   An allegation is an accusation. A person who is alleged to have committed a crime is accused of it but is innocent. If the allegation is proved in court, then the person is guilty of the crime.

appeal   Once convicted or found liable, a person may decide to ask for a higher court (the Supreme Court of Canada is the highest) to review the outcome of the trial. Sentences may also be appealed (presumably, the defence would argue that the sentence was too severe, the Crown that it was not severe enough). The only basis for an appeal is that the law has been applied incorrectly, not that the facts of the case were wrong. In other words, if the judge applied the law correctly to incorrect facts, then there is no basis for appeal. Appeals are not granted automatically, and a hearing must decide whether there are proper grounds for an appeal to be allowed.

arraignment   An accused person is brought into court to answer the charges. This is the formal accusation of the crime.

bail   A person accused of a crime can be held in jail until the trial or can be released by posting a bond (usually money or property) that is "held hostage" by the court to ensure that the accused shows up for the trial. A **bail hearing** is held after the arrest to decide whether bail should be granted and how much it should be to guarantee the person's appearance. Bail can be denied if it is feared that the accused won't show up for the trial or if the prosecution convinces the judge that setting the person free until the trial would pose a threat to public safety.

charge   A charge is an accusation made before a judge. It specifically names the crime or crimes that are alleged to have been committed by the accused.

Crown   The prosecution in Canada is called "the Crown" because a criminal trial is a confrontation between "the defence" (those representing the accused person to try to prove that the person is not guilty of the crime) and "the prosecution" (those representing the people or government of

Canada to try to prove that the accused person did the crime). Since the Queen is the head of government in Canada, the prosecution is said to represent the Crown.

felony This is an American term, not used in Canadian law. A serious crime such as murder, robbery, or assault results in a felony charge, while less serious crimes are "misdemeanors" in the United States. (See "Indictable Offence.")

hearing Any legal proceeding in court before a judge is called a hearing. It includes both a motion and a trial or an inquest.

homicide The culpable killing of one person by another is homicide, but Canadian law provides for different degrees of blame for killing. **First-degree murder** is planned or committed during the course of another crime; **second-degree** is unplanned; and **manslaughter** is accidental (though "voluntary" manslaughter is not accidental but not done with "wrongful intention").

indictable offence Such offences are the "major" crimes of murder, robbery, assault, et cetera. Lesser offences are called "summary conviction offences."

indictment Once the accused has been charged, it is still necessary to show that there is enough evidence that the person should stand trial for the offence. Once this has been determined, sometimes by a "preliminary hearing" before a "grand jury," in which the Crown must show that there is sufficient evidence to put the accused on trial, an indictment, or formal charge, is prepared, and that is what the trial is about.

jury In many cases, the parties have the right for the case to be tried before a jury, a group of people (12 in criminal cases, six in civil cases) randomly selected from the public. Both the defence and the Crown have the right to question prospective jurors to make sure they are impartial. The jury hears the trial and determines the facts to which the law is to be applied and then receives instructions about the law and rules from the judge. They then decide on the guilt or innocence of the accused person. A **hung jury** (slang) is one that cannot reach a decision about the case; such a situation can result in a **mistrial** and the selection of a new jury for a retrial.

In Canada, reporters may not talk to a juror (or the judge) about a trial during or after the case, and jurors are not supposed to reveal what went on in the jury room during a trial. This is not the case in the United States, and jurors have often appeared in the media after sensational trials.

parole People who have been sent to jail can be paroled or set free after serving parts of their sentences. Their freedom is conditional on their good behaviour while on parole (a **parole board**, which decides whether a criminal qualifies to be paroled, can also set specific conditions).

probation Instead of being sent to jail, a person found guilty of certain crimes can be given conditional freedom. The judge who decides to offer probation instead of a jail term can also set specific conditions, such as treatment for alcoholism, counselling to manage anger, or restrictions on associating with certain people. A person who breaches the terms of probation or commits an offence while on probation will have to fulfil the original penalty.

subpoena This is a court document that requires a person (or thing) to be present at a certain time and place, usually for a court proceeding. Witnesses can be subpoenaed to appear in court to give their testimony, and a reporter's notes or tapes can be subpoenaed as evidence.

suit A lawsuit is a claim by one person or group against another that is settled in court. A person may sue to recover money or to get compensation for injury (physical or emotional). Such trials are part of **civil law**, having to do with matters that do not involve criminal activity (which are dealt with under **criminal law**). Note that, while criminal law in Canada is consistent across the country, Quebec's civil law has been based on the French model since the 17th century. There are significant differences between Quebec's civil law and the British-based system used in the rest of the country.

Assignments

1. Attend your local town or city council meeting and prepare a report explaining the physical layout of the council chambers, the activities of the reporters who were there, the proceedings, and your overall impressions. Interview one or two veteran reporters to get advice and insight into reporting on city council.

2. Use the guidelines in Assignment 1 to prepare a report on court proceedings in the nearest courtroom.

10

Specialty Coverage

As part of normal news coverage, every station devotes some time to specialty news such as sports, weather, entertainment, and so on. The time and effort devoted to such special-interest news will depend on the station's demographics (who makes up its audience). A radio station that caters in its music selection and overall sound to a young, urban audience will emphasize sports and entertainment and probably not cover business or agriculture. A television station in rural Canada, east, central, or west, will feature agriculture but likely won't spend much time on traffic reports. Sports is often a beat assignment, which means the reporter covers nothing else. Entertainment, agriculture, traffic, weather, and other specialties, however, are sometimes just parts of a general reporter's daily responsibilities, especially at small stations; larger ones and, of course, networks can afford to devote full-time staff to these areas.

In general, covering news in any of these specialties requires no new skills or techniques that you wouldn't employ in covering more "mainstream" news stories. However, there are some sources, a few suggestions, and some pitfalls that we can talk about.

Sports

The primary requirement for a good sports reporter is to know the subject. People who tune in to sports reports are more knowledgeable about the subject than the audience for any other branch of the news. They know the people, the teams, the leagues, the plays, and the rules — and they expect expertise in the reports they see and hear.

This does not mean that a sports report should be a forum for a sports junkie to show off. A good sports report will fulfil the needs of a sports fan as well as provide understandable information and perhaps some insight for the less fanatic. People who go into sports reporting are often avid sports fans, some with encyclopedic knowledge of every aspect of every game; such people sometimes have a problem coming down to earth and conveying information to a broad audience without sounding obnoxious, superior, or just crazed. Some of the best sports reporters in Canada's electronic media are men and women who have come to sports after refining their skills in "hard" news. They bring objectivity, an ability to relate to an audience (fan and non-fan alike), and superior writing skills to the job, and these qualities, not their overenthusiasm for sports trivia, take them to the top.

Most sports information comes into the station from the wire services and is handled like any other wire copy: rewrite, localize, update. The best sports departments are those that cover local and regional sports with the same enthusiasm and skill as they cover national and international events. This requires legwork, getting out to the games, talking to the players, coaches, parents, and fans. It requires making and keeping contacts in the local sports scene.

Writing sports news presents several challenges. One is numbers. Sports seems sometimes to be more about numbers than people. Unless care is taken to present masses of numbers in a meaningful context, a sportswriter can overwhelm an audience. Another problem is repetition. There are only so many ways to say "won" or "lost," and yet those two words often seem to be all that sports is about. The other extreme, finding new and ridiculously inappropriate verbs to substitute, is equally hard to listen to: "Windsor annihilated Western, while St. Mary's massacred Alberta." Try to find an appropriate balance between the boring repetition of "beat" or "over" and the silly extremes of violent overkill. Finally, sportswriting is drowning in clichés. While some phrases have become a necessary part of the language, every sportswriter should try to find clear, creative, personal ways to express ideas instead of falling back on tired clichés that have been heard over and over for 50 years and more.

In covering sports events, it is always a good idea to find a compelling human angle to the story of teams and statistics and winners and losers. By focussing on individual hopes, accomplishments, tragedies, and triumphs, a sports reporter can lift coverage of a routine event into human drama that transcends sports and goes far beyond a traditional sports audience.

Weather

Weather information is sometimes the most important part of a newscast; it alone can be the reason that people tune in if a nasty storm, a heavy snowfall, or the possibility of rain after a long drought is in the forecast. While weather is a brief segment at the end of most radio newscasts, it is a significant segment of most TV news programs, and reporters who specialize in weather coverage are the rule.

The wire service is the source of most weather information in radio, with reports often fed in from Environment Canada or the meteorologist at the local airport. Television invests more money in weather resources, some stations even hiring their own meteorologist and buying radar and forecasting equipment.

As with all other coverage, it is important to be comfortable with the terminology and to sound as though you know what you're talking about. If you are assigned weather reporting, read up on it, learn all you can about frontal systems, pressure zones, and the influences on the weather in your area. By the way, good television weather reporters who have backgrounds in meteorology are much more in demand and usually make more money than other specialty reporters; some courses or even a degree in meteorology might be an investment that pays off in a broadcast career.

Besides the technology of weather reporting, TV weather forecasters must master the art of the chroma board. Looking comfortable in front of the board and pointing naturally to where you mean to point while looking at an off-camera monitor are skills that are developed with practice, but they're skills that are required. Much of the weather report is ad libbed or unscripted. Being able to talk easily and coherently about the weather without a full script is another skill that is valuable and requires that knowledge and thorough preparation we've talked about before. One intangible asset that successful weather reporters bring to their jobs is the ability to project personality. Weather people seem to be the most pleasant, the most likable, members of the news team. Stations want knowledgeable, skilful weather reporters, but they hire people with bright and engaging personalities. The ideal weather person will combine both aspects.

In writing weather copy, whether for TV or radio, remember to emphasize the local. Audiences are not interested in a frontal system moving across Ohio unless that system is causing weather disturbances in their neighbourhoods. Weather, above all other types of news, must be local to be of any interest. Also, a skilful writer will try to present the weather news in ordinary language with as little jargon and technical content as possible. Instead of saying "We expect light precipitation to resume overnight with a high probability of significant accumulations of up to ten centimetres by midafternoon tomorrow," put the sentence into conversational terms: "We'll get some light snow overnight, but it'll get heavier tomorrow morning, and by midafternoon there could be as much as ten centimetres on the ground."

Agriculture

Reporting news of specific interest to "agribusiness" is obviously a bigger priority in some areas than others. It is surprising, though, how many Canadians say the livestock reports and farm news broadcasts in urban centres are a part of their daily listening and viewing. In smaller towns and cities, and in large metropolitan areas that are closely aligned to agricultural activities, farm news is as important and as popular as weather reports.

In reporting on agriculture, the considerations that apply to other specialty types of reporting hold: know your material and localize the information. If you are not familiar with agricultural terminology, do some research and reading. Talk to agribusiness people and to professors or experts who work in agriculture. Subscribe to farm journals and get on the mailing list of the federal Department of Agriculture and your provincial ministry. If you demonstrate ignorance of the information you are conveying through mispronunciation, incorrect facts, omitted material, or even just hesitation due to unfamiliarity, your credibility with a very critical audience will be eroded.

To localize your reports, find out what is important to the farmers (and all the other workers who depend on agriculture) in your area and emphasize that. A report on prices paid per tonne for cherries or peaches at the cannery is not going to excite Saskatchewan grain farmers any more than a story about a breakthrough in oat yield per hectare is going to grab a Niagara or Okanagan fruit farmer. Go to local agricultural exhibitions and fall fairs, attend farm association meetings, stay in touch with clubs and groups concerned with agriculture — and report on all of them.

Farm reports do not have to consist only of the current prices for various livestock and produce that make up most of what comes over the wire. A good agriculture reporter will comb the "regular" news for agriculture-related stories, get interviews with farmers, politicians, producers, processors, even consumers. There is no reason that the daily agricultural news roundup can't be as interesting, creative, personal, and informative as everything else from the newsroom. There is a place in the newsrooms of most Canadian radio and TV stations for an agriculture specialist, even if that specialty is only part of an individual's responsibilities.

Other Specialties

Entertainment, business, religion, consumer affairs, health, education: all these subjects and many more are specialty reporting assignments at different television and radio stations. As we have seen, the most important aspects of specialty reporting are to be knowledgeable about your information and to localize it. For every specialty report, there is an audience that is informed, interested, and critical. Such people will not have much patience with reporters who do not take their valued subjects seriously, but they will make a hero of a reporter who provides thorough, local, interesting, and creative coverage of the field.

In a very competitive business, many broadcast rookies have found good jobs by demonstrating a willingness to specialize. By taking courses in agriculture, health, business, comparative religion, the environment, science, the arts, food and nutrition, early childhood education, tourism, and so on, beginning reporters can present a useful package to a prospective employer. Careers are made of specialty coverage: weather, business, and agriculture reporters on large stations and networks have been valued employees for many years. You can probably name several such individuals from your own watching and listening.

Sports is another story. So many young people want to be sports reporters that it takes a unique angle, an outstanding audition tape, or a lucky break to get into big-time sports reporting. Many sports reporters are former athletes who are recognized locally and who, presumably, have some broadcasting skills.

Assignments

1. Record as many different specialty reports as you can find in your broadcast area. Weather and sports are easy, but try to find stations that do a good job of news in entertainment, agriculture, business, religion, food, education, the environment, consumer affairs, children, the arts, or other specialties. Many such reports can be found on television more readily than on radio. Critique these reports. How do they differ from other news?

2. Read specialty sections of the newspapers. Clip good stories and rewrite them in broadcast style.

3. Do you have a hobby, an interest, or an area of expertise that you could sell to a station as a weekly 15-minute special? You will need to convince a program director or station manager that there is a significant audience for your show, that an advertiser will want to buy commercial time for it, that there is sufficient material for an interesting program every week — and that you are the person to produce it. Put together a one- or two-page proposal for such a program and include on cassette one sample show.

11

Rewriting

We covered the basics of writing broadcast news in Unit One, but here it is important to review those skills for the specific purpose of rewriting stories instead of creating a story from the facts. Rewriting is a very important part of the newswriter's job, in some cases consuming more time on a shift than writing original copy. There are really four reasons for rewriting: (1) to adapt writing that is meant for print into broadcast style; (2) to make corrections; (3) to change the wording and revise the content so the story sounds different for the next newscast; and (4) to localize and update existing stories.

Broadcast Stories

Once a story has been read on air, it should be rewritten before being used again. An audience hearing the same story over and over will quickly grow tired of it and, realizing that there is nothing new, tune out or switch stations. Frequently, a major story will lead radio newscasts for several hours in a row, and an audience that hears the same story in the same words will quickly become bored. For this reason, when a reporter covers an event, it is standard practice to write two or three or four versions of the story for use on different newscasts. Some versions may be lengthy and include inserts, while others might be short summaries for use on shorter newscasts.

Changing the order in which the facts are presented is a good rewriting technique, but the most important aspects of the story must not be buried for the sake of making the story sound different. Revising the wording and changing the sentence structure will also keep the material fresh. A less important detail might be dropped from one version or replaced with another minor fact. Here are two versions of the same story, written for subsequent hourly newscasts.

> There will be no strike at Freshaire Food Processors. The local union . . . representing the 150 employees of the food-packing company . . . announced this morning that an agreement has been reached with the company. President of the Food Handlers Union Local . . . Jenny Wyckemann . . . says the deal will mean a wage freeze for two years, but job security and working conditions have been improved. The workers have been without a contract since September and could legally strike next week.

> Workers at Freshaire Foods won't get a wage increase for two years . . . but they have avoided a strike. The 150 workers at the local food-processing plant could have been on strike as early as next week, but an agreement was reached early this morning. Union President Jenny Wyckemann says the deal means better working conditions and improved job security, and she will recommend acceptance by her union members in spite of the wage freeze.

Exercise 11.1

Write two broadcast stories for use in subsequent hourly newscasts for each of the following sets of facts. Don't forget to use everything you now know about good leads, broadcast style, and effective writing. Suggested approaches are discussed on page 232.

1. • Two men escaped from the Midvale medium security facility last night.
   • One is Henry White, aged 45, from near Edmonton, convicted of armed robbery and in his 3rd year of a 9-year sentence. The other is Victor Kropeci, 21, from Halifax, convicted of car theft and in his 2nd year of a 4-year sentence.
   • They got out by hiding in a food delivery truck, and their escape was noticed within half an hour.
   • They were caught at 4:30 a.m. by police and prison guards using tracking dogs in a heavily wooded area about 10 km from the prison.

2. • Heavy rains have caused the Little Crow Creek to flood its banks.
   • The town of Riverside has been evacuated because the hydroelectric dam on the Little Crow is threatened, and if it collapses a wall of water will hit Riverside.
   • Hydro officials are monitoring the water and the dam but say that so far there is no danger and that it's just a precautionary measure.

• Several farms north of the town are already under water, and two deaths are attributed to the flood.
• Damage is already over $5,000,000 and is expected to go much higher even if the dam holds.
• The forecast is for more rain and high winds over the next two days.

3. • Daryl Dalrymple, 61, and his son Denny, 33, were fishing on Halibut Lake yesterday from their boat the *Lucky Charm*.
• Daryl caught a sunfish that weighed 3.3 kilograms using a Mepps Aglia lure.
• They had it weighed at Horton's Hardware and took a picture before releasing it.
• It is believed to be a world record for this species. Ministry of Natural Resources officers are checking, and the *Guinness Book of World Records* has been contacted.
• Daryl says it's only the second time he's ever been fishing. The first time was almost 30 years ago.

Wire Service

The wire services employ well-qualified professionals to write and rewrite the material that comes into your station's computers over the satellite link. Many people think that the writing can't be improved, and that "rip and read" — taking the stories directly from the wire into the broadcast booth — is the way to go. There are three reasons to rewrite rather that use rip and read.

1. **To improve accuracy:** typos and other errors abound in the material printed from the wire.
2 **To add personality:** both the reader and the station have a "sound," a personality that is uniquely theirs (or they should have), and wire copy is generic, middle of the road, the same for everyone.
3. **To localize and update:** as we have seen, these comprise a vital part of a newswriter's duties and an important part of why people tune in to local radio and TV stations.

The wire service that comes into your station will be a broadcast service, but sometimes the material that comes over the wire is not rewritten from the print wire (stories meant for newspapers). This is another reason to use the wire copy as your starting point; then use your broadcast writing skills to improve on it for your own newscasts.

Sometimes, under the pressure of deadlines and the constant interruptions that are a normal part of newsroom activity, the most conscientious newspeople will resort to rip and read. This is natural, but a newswriter should use this practice as a last resort. Rewriting copy has so many benefits, among them the polishing of your broadcast writing skills, that it should be a priority. Here are two examples of real stories that came over the newswire in recent years — imagine yourself in the newsbooth with them in front of you because you decided to do a rip and read.

> Supporters of ousted Georgian leader Zviad Gamsakhurdia have agreed to negotiate a peaceful end to the country's civil conflict. They've been battling the supporters of the country's new government trying to. . . .

> The weather outside is still frightful from western Nortsf'cLOKvsc 1/4Lsftnd& 1/4 fgOnnfG1 7/8fHsLfOn 7/80 1/2ffyfLcLffNdwLwffFgLfy 7/8fyv Taxpayers have been left holding about 266 million dollars in costs for the facility. The private ownership group includes the Canadian Imperial Bank of Commerce, Ford of Canada, Coca-Cola Beverages, Controlled Media Communications. . . .

Exercise 11.2

Rewrite the following wire copy. Remember to correct all errors in style or writing, to add personality, and to localize and update wherever possible. Example answers begin on page 232.

1. People who suffer from rheumatoid arthritis appear to do best when they are treated within the first years of being stricken. A researcher says a study of people given a potent anti-rheumatic drug called methotrexate, as well as several other drugs, finds they had the greatest improvement when they were treated within five years of being diagnosed.

2. The German interior ministry says the number of people seeking asylum in Germany dropped to 323 thousand last year, compared to the year before. The decrease is thought to be linked to tighter laws . . . making it more difficult to claim asylum in Germany.

3. The woman charged with kidnapping baby Shelby from a Burlington hospital just before Christmas is wanted in two U.S. states. Halton Regional Police Detective Doug Ford says there are arrest warrants for Hill in Oklahoma and Michigan, but he won't say exactly what they relate to. Ford does note that the warrants have nothing to do with the kidnapping case here. 43-year-old Hill, a former resident in Michigan, is charged with kidnapping five-day-old Shelby Walsh from Joseph Brant Hospital two weeks ago. The child was taken by a woman posing as a hospital worker. The little girl was found unharmed about 11 hours later in a nearby motel.

4. A former police officer saved the life of a heart attack victim this morning. Gerard Lavoie, 61, collapsed while shopping with his wife in Parkview Mall. Luckily, former RCMP sergeant Howard Schmidt happened to be nearby and applied lifesaving techniques to revive Lavoie. He was taken to St. Joseph's Hospital, where his condition is listed as satisfactory. Schmidt retired from the force two years ago after a 26-year career. He says this is the first time he's ever had to use the CPR training he had in the Mounties.

5. A strong winter storm that dumped heavy snow across the central states and the northeast has left thousands of would-be travellers stranded in Florida. Airports from Pittsburgh to Boston were closed overnight or operated on reduced schedules. Airlines hope to resume most flights later today, but passengers are advised to check exactly when their flights will be leaving. The weather also disrupted other travel. Some interstate highways have been closed because of ice or drifting snow. And rail traffic is just getting back to speed following delays due to icy tracks.

Newspapers

As already noted, there are instances when broadcast newswriters want to adapt newspaper stories for use in their newscasts. We know that newspaper writing is inappropriate for broadcast, so such stories must be completely rewritten. In addition, remember that it is illegal and unethical to use stories from newspapers without acknowledging the sources. Once you have checked the story independently, added your own information, obtained taped inserts, and rewritten it, the story is yours and may be used without acknowledgement.

News Releases

Great care must be taken in rewriting news releases — and they *must* be rewritten, never broadcast as submitted. News releases are used to get across a specific point of view or promote a specific agenda. In many cases, the person or organization issuing the release hopes to use the news media to publicize this point of view or agenda — almost like a free advertisement.

The first question that a newswriter must ask when confronted with a news release is "Is this news?" If there is a legitimate reason that your listeners and viewers might need or want to know the information in the release, then you can proceed to rewrite it. Eliminate all material that is clearly biased or self-serving. Regard all adjectives with suspicion. Whenever a fact is unfamiliar or seems questionable to you, check it independently. Once you have broadcast this story, your audience will hold you, not the author of the news release, accountable for its accuracy. Usually, the name of a contact person is included with the release; this person might be a good source for a preliminary check but is likely the person who wrote the news release in the first place.

Often a news release is a good beginning, nothing more. It can point you in the direction of a story that you will have to research, check, and produce. The finished story, the *real* news, may have almost nothing to do with the original news release that dropped on your desk.

Here are a news release that came into a station and the story that was eventually broadcast.

NEWS RELEASE
FOR IMMEDIATE USE

At a meeting held last night, the Environmental Action Party (EAP) voted unanimously to condemn the building of an extension to 44th St. across Trout Creek. After hearing a report from Professor Calvin Higgins, a world-renowned expert in urban planning and environmental impact, members of the party agreed to begin a concerted campaign to put a halt to the proposed extension.

"The impact on wildlife living in and around the creek and its surrounding wetlands will be nothing short of catastrophic," said Professor Higgins. He also pointed out that the extension was unnecessary since a widening of the existing roadways at Duke St. and 42nd St. would accomplish the same thing.

President of the EAP, Tania Roberto, pledged the resources of the party and its more than 50 local members to fighting the project. "It is our responsibility as concerned citizens of this city, and, indeed, this planet, to stop such irresponsible and thoughtless over-development," Ms. Roberto stated.

CONTACT: TANIA ROBERTO
DEPARTMENT OF BIOLOGY, NORTHERN UNIVERSITY

This is the report broadcast.

A local environmental group is going to fight City Hall over the proposed extension of 44th Street. The Environmental Action Party . . . a group formed last year by students in the Department of Biology of Northern University . . . says that the extension is unnecessary and threatening to wildlife. At a meeting last night, the 50-member organization voted to try to stop the project. Environmental Action Party President Tania Roberto says the group will use every legal means at their disposal, but she would not rule out confrontation if the extension goes ahead. The 44th Street extension proposal has passed the City Planning Committee and goes before council next week for debate.

Updating

Updating is one of the newsroom's routine jobs. Once a story has been broadcast, newswriters should immediately begin thinking of how it can be made fresh. Research is necessary to get a new angle, a reaction, voice or visuals, or further detail or background, or to stay on top of changing events. As already noted, police and hospital checks will determine if charges have been laid, bail hearings set, arrests made, names released, or if the conditions of people who were hurt have changed.

For example, you might be told of a major car accident in an early morning police check. At first, you might be told only that it's a PI (personal injury) and that charges are pending. Throughout the day, you and your newsroom colleagues will find, through frequent checks, the names of the people hurt, their medical conditions, the nature of the charges, the names of those charged, and details of the accident. It may take all day before all the information is available. Follow-up in later days and weeks will provide updates on the conditions of the victims and the progress of the accused person's trial from arraignment to acquittal or conviction and sentencing.

Another important aspect of updating is getting reaction. Once a story is broadcast, those whom it affects should be contacted to get their opinions or points of view. For the news release above, for example, it might be useful to get the reactions of city planners. Will the extension really cause environmental damage? Is another route possible, and would it save the taxpayers money? One form of reaction that is interesting, but should not be overused, is the person-on-the-street (POS) interview. Random voice or visual clips of ordinary people's reactions to a well-publicized event can add a dimension to your coverage. Remember, however, that such random samplings mean nothing statistically. A sample of at least 100, with carefully worded questions and control conditions, is necessary before any statistical validity is possible, so POS interviews should not be given great importance: they are merely samples of the opinions your microphone happened to catch.

Exercise 11.3

List at least five sources of information you would go to in order to update each of the following stories. Share your ideas with others, and see how many ideas emerge; the ability to identify good updating and localizing sources is a very valuable skill.

1. A robbery at a convenience store last night. Clerk was hit over the head and sent to hospital. Two hundred dollars taken from the cash register, two customers robbed of jewellery and about 100 dollars cash. Two people arrested, another being sought. Fifth convenience store holdup in this area in the past month.

2. Accident at local metal-fabricating plant this morning. One worker killed, name not released, two others hurt and in hospital. Explosion and fire believed to have been caused by careless storage of chemicals. Firefighters took four hours to control the fire, one treated for smoke inhalation, another for chemical burns. Fire marshal's office is investigating.

3. Professor at local college accused of sexual harassment after complaints by five students. Professor Douglas McTammany suspended with pay until case is heard by human rights board at the college. Professional association is defending McTammany, students' union is pressing charges on behalf of the students. So far, no criminal charges have been laid, police not involved, purely an internal college matter.

Localizing

Proximity — a connection with your audience's home area — is one of the most important news values. Any story that has it is significantly enhanced. Any time that an international story involves large numbers of Canadians, there may be some local content. One of those Canadians might be a neighbour, co-worker, relative, or classmate of some of the people tuning in to your newscast.

Sometimes imaginative research turns up local angles. It's often a matter of thinking creatively: "Where can I check to see if local people are involved in this event?" If the story is travel related, for example (an air tragedy, tourists stranded by a storm, foreigners caught in a sudden revolution or riot), call local travel agents, who will have passenger lists. Once you find that a local person is involved, can you get in touch with that person for an interview? Has he or she phoned home and left a number? If Canadian

Armed Forces personnel are involved, their names and addresses might be available from the local recruiting office or regional headquarters. National sports teams, arts organizations, competitors of all kinds can be checked at the head office of the organization (though an alert news staff would already know when local people are involved in such high-profile events).

One useful way to localize distant events is to get local expert commentary. Many stations keep lists of local people who have expertise in a variety of international areas so that when a story breaks the local person can be contacted for voice and visuals. Teachers, especially college and university professors, are very useful for such expert commentary since most post-secondary institutions have international studies departments as well as people whose research has taken them overseas.

Exercise 11.4

Suggest at least three local sources that you could contact to localize each of the following stories. Share your answers with others to develop creative networks of local contacts.

1. A freak snowstorm in Florida has caused millions of dollars in damage. All air transport grounded, roads closed.
2. Canadian chefs have won international cooking competition in Lyon, France. Team of 12 chefs from all parts of Canada competed against teams from 55 other countries in seven different competitions, including appetizers, desserts, breakfasts, vegetable dishes, and one complete gourmet meal.
3. General Motors, Ford, and Chrysler report sales of over ten and a half million vehicles last year, an increase of eight percent from the year before. Light trucks had the biggest increase, with sport-utility vehicles and subcompacts also doing well. Full-size luxury cars slumped in sales.

Assignment

Begin to make your own contact list of people who could be useful as sources for any story or situation that arises. Use index cards or a Rolodex, and with each name and telephone number list the area of expertise or authority of the person. Whenever you use that person as a source or in an interview, note the date and subject on the card. It is also a good idea to cross-index the file according to subject so that if you need information on South Africa, but can't remember who your best source is, you can look up South Africa and find the name. You will have to begin a new contact file for each location your career takes you to, but by beginning one now you will learn where the best contacts can be found and how best to structure your file so that it's useful and accessible.

Unit Three
Review Exercises

Review 3.1

Write three different versions of this story for use on subsequent hourly newscasts.

- Workers excavating a basement for a parking garage on the edge of the downtown area have discovered ancient artefacts.
- Archeologists from Northern University say the find is very significant, and they may need as long as ten years to fully explore the site, thought to be a complete village more than two thousand years old.
- Developers of the garage site, S-P-M Developments, say they are losing almost 100 thousand dollars every day that the project is delayed, and they will go to court to get permission to proceed.
- The site was found two days ago when a backhoe operator brought fragments of pottery and bones to the surface with his shovel, but it has been kept secret until now so the area could be sealed off.
- Government officials had previously checked the site for environmental and historical impact and had given the okay for the development.

Review 3.2

List ten people or organizations you would go to for more information, interviews, reactions, or follow-up on the story in Review Exercise 3.1

Review 3.3

Rewrite this press release to make it acceptable for broadcast.

The Palm Lake Liberal Association is pleased to announce that its candidate in the next provincial election will be an outstanding citizen and community leader, Mrs. Vivien Cartier. "Viv," as she is known in the community, has managed Cartier Real Estate for eleven years, is the past president of the Chamber of Commerce, and has been an active and respected member of town council for the past three terms. She is a member of the Palm Lake Baptist Church, on the executive of the Rotary Club, and an active member of the Royal Palm Curling Club. Mrs. Cartier's vision for the future is of a strong province unburdened by debt and with full employment. She enjoys the full and unqualified support of the other candidates who ran for the nomination, Mayor Bob Denniston and Shelagh McCormick. The Palm Lake Liberal Association welcomes support from thoughtful and responsible voters. Please call 661-116-6111 with your pledge of time or money to help elect Vivien Cartier.

Review 3.4

List five people you would like to talk to in order to follow up the story in
Review Exercise 3.3.

UNIT 4
Delivery

Introduction

Electronic journalism is still a relatively young business, and styles of delivery are evolving. In the earliest days of broadcast, almost any voice or appearance was acceptable. Newspaper reporters frequently made the transition to radio and television, not because they had good voices or authoritative appearances, but because there was an assumption that whatever made them good newspaper people would make them equally good radio and television news reporters and newsreaders. Then the pendulum of what is acceptable swung to the other extreme, and newsreaders and reporters were hired for appearance and voice quality alone, with no thought for their understanding of, knowledge about, or consideration for the news they were delivering. The wonderful film *Broadcast News* thoughtfully skewers this attitude of newsperson as performer only.

Now there seems to be a more realistic concept of the newsperson. While there are still some holdouts and carryovers from the days of the news being delivered only by fabulously rich and resonant voices and attractive, commanding faces, content and the newsperson's expertise and ability are now as important as sound and appearance. We are seeing more visible minorities on TV, hearing more accents on the radio, and why shouldn't we? Our news media should reflect our society, not some Barbie and Ken ideal that exists only in the mind of a casting agent. Good journalists are regularly heard and seen on the air, even if sometimes they have less than perfect features and voices that are pleasant and clear though not deep and dramatic. We are also hearing a more natural style of delivery. The heavily emphatic and cadenced delivery that made even the most mundane news dramatic has been largely replaced by a more conversational and natural presentation.

Even though more variation in the sound and appearance of the newscaster is becoming common, this does not mean that every station will hire the first person who applies for a reading or reporting job. Competition for these positions is fierce, and stations are going to hire the people who can serve their audiences best. An accent, if it does not interfere with clarity and understanding, may not be a barrier in itself, but if it is combined with a sloppy reading style, careless preparation, an untrained voice, or any number of other defects, there is ample reason for a news director to hire someone else. In other words, good on-air presentation is not entirely the product of heredity and luck anymore: with training, effort, and practice, most people who want to can make themselves acceptable newsreaders.

12

Preparation

Under the pressure of deadlines, the precious time available before a newscast is often spent in gathering, writing, editing, and producing the stories rather than in preparation for their delivery. This is a mistake. The best-researched, most beautifully written, elegantly edited, and lavishly produced story can be destroyed by a poor on-air presentation. Reporters and news anchors alike must factor in as much time as possible to prepare for the read. Credibility is at stake; a newsreader who does not sound authoritative, confident, and knowledgeable loses believability. The audience realizes that this person is just reading from a page. As we have already noted, and will note again, the audience wants news delivered by people perceived to be the most able to provide the facts, the truth — not just actors hired to read a script. Without credibility as a knowledgeable, authoritative source of information, a newsreader, even one with "great pipes," has nothing.

Under hectic conditions, preparation must consist of *at least* one careful read through. Time should also be scheduled to permit pronunciation checks and careful copy marking. Ideally, a full rehearsal is part of the preparation, but seldom is there time for this luxury.

Copy Check

As a minimum, read through the copy you are about to deliver—carefully, fully, and *aloud*. Spelling errors, typos, hard-to-pronounce words or names, peculiar sentence structure, or confusing wording should be noted, corrected, or marked so that you won't stumble or sound tentative during the newscast. An understanding of the basic content is necessary so that your delivery is consistent with the nature of the story. Newscasters who have not had the time for a read through have been known to burst into laughter on air because they read an unexpectedly amusing story. Others have begun to read a story they assume is a "kicker" or amusing human interest story only to change tone in mid-story as they realize they're reading about a tragedy.

The following stories were handed to newsreaders to deliver on air. Had they not first been carefully checked and corrected, they would have made it difficult for the reader to maintain composure and credibility.

> The Leafs blanked the Caps last night 3-0. The Leafs dominated play through most of the game, scoring one in the first and two in the second. The Capitals couldn't get untracked until the third, when they got their only goal.

> A PC member of the legislature is under investigation for election irregularities. Harvey McMinnis has admitted to the party caucus that police are checking into his spending diring the last election inoctober. Police are not saying anything about the nature of the investigation is the second time that questions have been asked about the Toty backbeacher's election practices.

Pronunciation

The most serious error a newsreader or reporter can make in delivering a story (short of breaking up in the middle of it) is mispronouncing words or names with which the audience is familiar. It is not acceptable for a professional newsperson to mispronounce even names that are unfamiliar to the audience. They may not catch you now, but later, when they have heard the correct pronunciation on another station or by another reader, some will remember that your pronunciation was wrong. However, your audience will know instantly when you have flubbed the names of local people (politicians, school board members, businesspeople, judges, lawyers, etc.) and places (street names, neighbouring communities, businesses, geographic features, etc.) To mispronounce these important names is simply unforgivable. Good newspeople will make themselves familiar as quickly as possible with all the local names and places in a new location. When an unfamiliar name appears, they will immediately check it with someone who knows its correct pronunciation.

Never guess! This is just laziness, and, even if you guess right once, you will not guess right every time. Even names that seem to be straightforward can lead to difficulty and should be confirmed. When Gilbert Parent became the speaker of the House of Commons, there was a flurry of phone calls to the local news organizations in his home riding: was his name to be pronounced in the English or French manner? How do you pronounce

Smythe? Some people prefer [SMITH], while some prefer [SMYE-th]. Is Bernstein pronounced [BERN styne] or [BERN steen]? Some prefer one, some the other.

In dealing with foreign names, there are several considerations. Always post the wire service pronouncers that are sent out regularly. They have been checked and confirmed, so you can be confident that these guidelines are accurate. If the name does not appear on the wire service pronouncer, check with someone who is originally from the same area as the person whose name is giving you difficulty (such people should be in the Rolodex of an alert newsroom). In all cases of non-English names, there is the question of whether to pronounce them as they are pronounced in the foreign language or to anglicize them. Most news organizations aim for accuracy without indulging in non-English pronunciations such as the rolling r's found in French or the throaty k's found in Arabic; get as close as you can to the authentic pronunciation without using non-English sounds, even if you are fluent in the language concerned.

As for English words that cause pronunciation difficulties, be aware of the most common and memorize them now. Any time that you question your pronunciation, look the word up in a dictionary and be guided by the pronunciation given there.

Exercise 12.1

The following list is an incomplete catalogue of troublesome common words and names. Look them up in a dictionary and write out a pronouncer beside each. To this list add your own troublesome words as you come across them.

arctic	grievous	mayoral(ty)
admirable	harass(ment)	mischievous
athlete	horror	modern
Belgrade	impotent	Newfoundland
climatic	indictment	nuclear
coma	infamous	preferable
comparable	inquiry	prescription
corps	Iran(ian)	probably
different	irreparable	ration
docile	Italian	realtor
environment	Kenya	recognize
epitome	kilometre	regime
February	Kuwait	status
forte (strength)	library	superfluous
Galapagos	lieutenant	usually
genuine	literature	vehicle (vehicular)

Emphasis

It is very difficult to teach correct emphasis in reading news stories. It is something that every reader must develop through experience and through listening to others. Essentially, emphasis means stressing certain words in a sentence with your voice, not just saying those words more loudly but also giving them "weight" or power. It is a combination of volume, pronunciation, and pausing. The objective is always to make the story easier to understand; the audience is the first consideration in knowing which words to emphasize and when to pause. How can I make this sentence clear, understandable? How can I get the meaning and importance of this sentence across? You do so by carefully selecting words that need emphasis. Consider the differences in meaning in these sentences when the capitalized word is emphasized.

> POLICE say the man is being held for questioning in the murder investigation.
> (Others have another opinion.)
>
> Police SAY the man is being held for questioning in the murder investigation.
> (But another reason for his being held is possible.)
>
> Police say the man is being held for QUESTIONING in the murder investigation.
> (They're just questioning him; he's not under arrest.)
>
> Police say the man is being held for questioning in the MURDER investigation.
> (They're questioning him in the murder investigation only.)

Some beginning newscasters know the importance of emphasizing words but don't connect the emphasis to the *meaning* of what they are reading, so they emphasize words almost randomly, and the result is a sing-song rhythm that is very unattractive and robs the stories of any true meaning. The best way to develop the skill of emphasizing words appropriately is to read your copy aloud. A natural, conversational emphasis is a good guideline. Which words would I emphasize if I were telling this story to my friends? Another useful practice in learning which words to emphasize is to listen closely to newscasters whose delivery you admire and tune in carefully to the emphasis they give.

One hint about effective delivery before we leave emphasis: nearly all beginning newsreaders make the mistake of *under*emphasizing the words they read. Effectively read news is overemphasized. Words to be emphasized are hammered into the microphone because the hardware of electronic media flattens the emphasis from the time you speak until the sound hits the listener's ear. If you don't exaggerate your read, you will sound flat, dull, and uninvolved with the stories. Although you may think you sound ridiculous as you overplay every word, the opposite is true: you sound normal. The proof is easy to obtain: record yourself. Practise reading stories on tape and play them back, listening critically.

Exercise 12.2

Practise emphasizing appropriate words by underlining the words in the sentences below that you think should be stressed. The answers, beginning on page 233, are suggestions of one standard approach at trying to increase clarity and meaning.

1. There are new allegations of corruption in the upper levels of city government. Documents recently obtained under the Freedom of Information legislation show that as much as one and a half million dollars is unaccounted for.
2. The coach stressed that no one would be benched until tomorrow night's game against the first-place Fangs. He admitted, however, that some drastic action may be needed to get the team back on track.
3. Today is the second anniversary of this city's worst snowstorm. More than half a metre of snow fell in less than six hours, knocking out electricity and shutting down the entire region. The forecast for today is mild by comparison.
4. A local resident is in serious condition at City Hospital after the car she was driving was hit by a slow-moving train. Witnesses say the woman's car stalled on the tracks at the Fifth Street railway crossing just as the eastbound freight pulled away from the yard.
5. China's government announced today that it would be raising domestic airfares by as much as 50 percent. The increase comes as a result of that country's move to a freer market economy and the necessity to compete on the world market for fuel and equipment.

Pacing

Pacing is the speed of delivery — how quickly or slowly the words in the newscast are read. To be effective, a story should be read at a variable pace, with some words run more quickly together and others separated by pauses. Pacing is a part of the technique used to provide emphasis and to make meaning clearer. A writer can provide some clues for the newsreader about appropriate places to pause by using ellipses, but writers should use such devices sparingly, when there is no alternative way to read the sentence. Emphasis and pacing must be left mostly up to the reader's individual style.

Overall, however, a newscast should have a "sound" that suits the sound of the station (see Chapter 14). On some stations, a fast, loud read is appropriate to the rock music, frantic commercials, and manic announcers-operators that make up the rest of the programming. You would sound out of place if your newscast was slow, dignified, and deliberate. The ability to adapt pace to situation is a skill that is developed over time and with practice. As a rule, most beginners try to read too quickly. Because they are well prepared and have read the stories over several times, they are able to gallop through them at a breakneck pace. Nervousness contributes to this speed. Slow down. Deliberately pause and emphasize the words you have marked. As with emphasis, you may think you sound terrible, but if you play back your newscast you will often find that you could have slowed down some more!

Another important aspect of pacing is being able to deliver an entire newscast within the time allotted for it. You must learn to time your delivery accurately so that you can arrange a newscast lineup with the correct amount of material to fill the exact time provided in the station's schedule. Your own speed of reading and the style of delivery favoured by the station will influence this amount, but as a guideline most newsreaders figure on between four and five seconds per line of standard-sized, typed copy. A ten-line story, then, would take between 40 and 50 seconds, depending on your reading speed. When you have an accurate idea of your pace, you can work it out in "seconds per line" to help you gauge how many stories you can fit into a newscast. Learn to judge quickly and accurately the time it will take you to read material and to assemble newscasts that will come out within a few seconds of the time provided.

Copy Marking

Now that we know we must (1) read our copy carefully to avoid the pitfalls of poorly written material or mistakes, (2) check pronunciation, (3) consider where to put emphasis, and (4) be conscious of pacing and deliberately insert appropriate pauses, how can we amend the copy we are to read so that all this comes across when we are on the air? Every newsreader takes a pen and marks up the copy before going to air with it. Different readers use different markings to remind them of how to read the material. You may want to develop your own copy-marking techniques, but those presented here are clear, easy, and fairly common in newsrooms.

While clear symbols and occasional corrections make copy easier to read, keep pencilled amendments to a minimum; a page that is too marked up becomes confusing and dangerous to try on the air. Rewrite pages that are getting cluttered or messy. Spelling errors are corrected by completely stroking through the word that contains the mistake and carefully printing the corrected word directly above it. This technique is used for any word that must be replaced (another reason for double or triple spacing all copy).

In Ottawa today, the minister of ~~Revenue~~ *finance* announced plans for a tax reduction.

When several words are to be omitted, stroke them out completely and draw a line from the word before the erasure to connect with the next word to be read.

There is, ~~according to the weather office,~~ a winter storm warning in effect this evening.

To insert a word, put the insert sign (^) where the word is to be added and print the word above the line.

The trial of Barbara Kraymore will ^*begin* on Thursday unless a further delay is granted.

To indicate a slight pause in the delivery, use a slash (/). Where a longer pause or complete stop is essential, use two slashes (//). Underline words that are to get emphasis.

A huge increase in the price of <u>coffee</u> is predicted, / as much as <u>50 percent,</u> / as a result of the poor harvests in Brazil and Colombia // The two main coffee-producing countries were hit by <u>heavy</u> <u>rains</u> and <u>flooding</u> just before harvest last year.

Pronouncers are words that are phonetically spelled, with the emphasized syllable capitalized and contained in square brackets [BRAK-ets]. Phrases that should get less emphasis because they are asides are put in parentheses. Words or phrases that are unfamiliar to listeners and should be given pronunciation emphasis are highlighted with large quotation marks.

The mayor, (his re-election plans still indefinite,) refused to take a stand on the issue, /and <u>instead</u> referred the matter to the standing sub-committee on policy and procedures.//

Before you go on the air, your copy might look like this.

Economists for Statistics Canada in Ottawa are predicting the country's <u>jobless rate</u>, (now ten point seven percent,) will hold at current levels. ‖The new <u>official</u> rate won't be released until Friday, /but StatsCan officials say they see <u>little</u> chance of a big change from <u>last</u> month's figure. ‖In <u>addition</u>, the agency predicts there's <u>not</u> going to be <u>any</u> change in the <u>inflation rate</u> this month either.

British Columbia is in for a <u>massive earthquake</u> . . . sometime in the next <u>200 years</u>. ‖Scientists at the Pacific Geo-Science Centre near Victoria say that <u>pressure</u> is building in the tectonic plates west of Vancouver Island, /and an earthquake of <u>giant proportions</u> is the inevitable result. ‖Garry Rogers, (head of earthquake studies at the Centre,) says that <u>Nanaimo</u>, <u>Victoria</u>, <u>Vancouver</u>, and all the communities along the <u>Fraser Valley</u> would be affected. ‖He called the event <u>potentially</u> <u>catastrophic.</u>

Exercise 12.3

Use a pencil to do your own copy marking for the following stories. Read them aloud and revise your marks to produce the best possible read; then record the result and analyze your performance. Do you need to exaggerate your emphasis more? Pause longer? Slow the pace? Try to improve your read until you have a version that is "perfect." Time this version and make note of your average "seconds per line" so that you can begin to develop accurate timing for your newscasts. This is the way to develop the habits and techniques that are necessary to produce a good read every time within the time constraints imposed by most newsrooms.

1. A local man makes the best pizza in Canada. At a competition held this week in Windsor, Ontario, Georgio DellaRiva beat almost 200 other competitors to take the top horours. DellaRiva owns Georgio's Gelateria and Pizza on River Road, where every day he offers the same pizza that was judged the country's best. The winning entry was a thin-crust pesto, tomato, and mushroom dish that Georgio says he learned to make from his mother, Antonia. The competition, which is sponsored every year by a cheese company, is supported by a cheese company and draws entries form every province. Georgio's prize for taking top prize is an all-expenses-paid trip to Italy and a large trophu, which he says will be proudly displayed in the entrance to his restaurnat.

2. Students at Hilltop College are angry about administration plans to raise their tuitions next year. A group of about 150 studnets gathered in front of the college today for a raily to protest the fee hike. The spokesman for the group, Dennis Hervey, said that the proposed increase of almost 200 dollars per semester would put a college education out of the reach of many young people already stretched to the limit. With few summer jobs available, the provincial grant program cancelled, and loans harder and harder to get, he said this extra money would be the last straq. The students waved plackards and chanted slogans for about an hour and then dispersed to go bakc ot classes. According to organizers of the protest, more action is planned.

3. A computer malfunction that interrupted phone service over a large part of downtown is being blamed on a hungry rodent. Workers rushed to the transfer station on Peart Avenue yesterday afternoon at about 2, when telephones went dead. They manged to restore service in a few inutes, using a backup system, but the investigation into the cause has taken until this morning. An embarassed telephone company representative told the media that the sabateur had been found . . . a field mouse. The mouse had eaten through a portective cable covering and then gnawed its way into one of the computer's main communications

lines, snorting the system. A hungry cat has been sent in to the transfer station to to eliminate the problem.

4. Firefighters are still dousing the embers of a fire that destroyed a city landmark today. The Connors building at the corner of Main and King Streets was built in 1895 and survived an earthquake, two fires, and an attempt by developers to tear it down for a high-rise apartment complex. This morning it is a smoking ruin. Three fire stations were involved in the attempt to save the building overnight after the first alarm was called in a 10 last night. Hampered by high winds, the firefighters could do nothing but prevent the spread of the blaze to neighbouring buildings. The Connors building housed a branch of the Royal Bank, an insurance company, as well as three floors of offices. No injuries have been reported, and no estimate of damage estimate is available yet.

5. Cities in England and Australia are already beginning to prepare their bids to host the Commonweath Games in 2006. Manchester, which lost out on its attempt to host the 2000 Olympics to Sydney, Australia, is competing against Sheffield and London. A Commonwealth Games Council will decide on England's representative. Meanwhile, Melbourne and Perth in Australia are showing interest in hosing the games. The Commonwealth Games Federation makes the final decision.

Assignment

Practice will make you a better reader, and, whether your aim is to be an anchor or a reporter, having a clearer, more confident and authoritative delivery will make you better at your job. Spend five minutes every day reading into a tape recorder. It doesn't matter what you read, but make the effort to read dramatically, with emphasis and feeling. Prepare for reading by checking the pronunciation of unfamiliar words and names and by copy marking to give correct emphasis and pacing to your read. Save your tapes so that you can chart your improvement. (In Chapter 13, you'll learn about warming up your voice and getting physically prepared for reading aloud; these exercises should be incorporated into your daily tape-recorded routine as well.)

13

Performance

Many people are attracted to broadcast journalism by the notion that they have great voices, which usually means deep, resonant, and authoritative voices. Such a voice can be an advantage in getting an on-air job; however, lesser voices can be trained and improved, and the greatest voices can often be made better. One broadcast veteran with more than 30 years of on-air experience in several of Canada's largest markets (and a voice that most broadcasters would die for) was still taking voice lessons in his 50s, and was still amazed and delighted by what he was learning about improving the quality, creativity, and range of his voice.

The voice and its development and improvement comprise the subject of many good books (one of which is *Voice and Diction* by Jon Eisenson, published by Maxwell Macmillan, Toronto, in 1992) and many postsecondary courses. Your college likely has such courses, perhaps disguised as drama or theatre arts offerings, public speaking, presentation skills, or some such course. Anyone who is planning on a career in the broadcast field, in which the voice is so much a part of success, should not ignore any opportunity to learn more about his or her capabilities and to expand them. Here we will only touch the surface and look at some ideas and exercises that can improve your delivery at this early stage in your career.

Breathing

When reading, it is necessary to have enough breath to read words at a consistent level and volume until you reach a natural pause in the material. Then you can inhale sufficient air to get you to the next natural stop. When news copy has been well marked (see Chapter 12), it is much easier to judge how long it will be until the next breath. Of course, the more words you can read on a breath (keeping the level and volume consistent and the sound natural), the more flexibility you have in where you can pause. This does not mean that the best way to proceed is to inhale as much air as possible and hold it while trying to get through a whole paragraph. What is important is that you can sustain a quality sound in your voice until the natural end of a phrase. The trick is to "preread" the copy in order to anticipate a pause. This means using your peripheral vision to scan the line ahead of where you are reading — not an easy skill to master, but one that you should practise consciously every time you read.

Abdominal breathing is the technique preferred by voice teachers for all public speaking, from poetry readings, to political speechmaking, to reading the news. As you sit in your chair, spread the fingers of both hands across your stomach just under your rib cage. When you inhale, your hands should rise; when you exhale, they should settle back down. If this process is reversed, then you are breathing with the top of your lungs and will have less breath available for reading, and your voice will sound thin and strained. Always practise abdominal breathing when you are reading aloud.

Most people can recite the letters of the alphabet to about H on a natural, conversational inhalation. This is sufficient for most purposes, as long as natural pauses in the material are not too far apart. Newsreaders should try to develop the ability to go farther than H. With practice, you should be able to recite the entire alphabet naturally, easily, without sounding at all strained and without changing the sound of your voice.

Exercise 13.1

These exercises are not "one time only" routines. A ten- to-15-minute session every day will produce significant results in your ability to read naturally, easily, and without even being conscious of your breathing.

1. Sit in a chair and place your fingers over your stomach (as described above). Breathe in, making sure that your hands rise as you do so, for five seconds. Make your exhalation last for ten seconds. Practise until this five-second-in, ten-second-out routine is easy and natural. Now, on the exhalation, push in with your fingers to force more breath out, letting the exhalation go on as long as you can without discomfort. You should be able to make your exhalation last about 30 seconds. Now practise the same thing, but on the exhalation make a clear, sustained "ah" sound. Do not change the volume or sound of the "ah" throughout the exhalation. Finally, try the silent exhalation first and then the vocal exhalation with your hands on the desk in front of you. Concentrate on making your abdominal muscles do the work of your fingers.

2. Using the techniques in Exercise 1, try reciting the alphabet or the months of the year as you exhale. While keeping your voice even and unstrained, try to increase the number of letters or months you can recite. Try this with both an easy, conversational inhalation and a big inhalation. Try it whispering (which, you will find, takes more breath than speaking aloud).

3. Read the following sentences aloud, pausing where indicated. Pause whether you need to breathe or not, but take a breath if you need to only in a marked pause.
   a. Police now believe that the woman's injuries were caused by an attacker // rather than from natural causes as was earlier suspected.
   b. The government of China is sending a trade delegation to Canada // with the purpose of encouraging more Canadian investment in China's underdeveloped northwest.
   c. More than half of the traffic fatalities in this city during the past year involved pedestrians, // and more than half of those pedestrians were over the age of 60, // according to statistics released today.
   d. The new plant will open within six months and at full capacity is expected to employ about 100 people in the production of consumer electronics // for both the domestic and the export markets.
   e. The prime minister is flying to Britain, // where he will meet with the British prime minister and the queen // before carrying on to Paris for a week-long tour leading up to the francophone summit.

Pitch

Most men and women who read the news on radio and television still have relatively deep voices; however, as we have noted, a pleasant, clear voice of any pitch can be eligible for on-air jobs. The reason that a low-pitched voice has always been favoured is the sound of authority it gives, a sound that is valuable in a newscaster, who must be credible and authoritative above all else. Many radio and TV performers, both in the news and in other aspects of the industries, who were not born with "great pipes" tried to lower their pitch through exercises and other means; some even took up smoking in the mistaken belief that doing so would lower their voices.

Everyone has a natural "pitch range" from the highest pitch her or his vocal chords can attain through to the lowest pitch achievable. Within this range, most people have a pitch where they are most comfortable, an "optimum pitch" for their physiology. Some people, however, frequently employ a pitch that is outside their optimum level; such people sound strained, and frequently their voices sound tired because their "habitual pitch" — the pitch they most often use — is not their optimum pitch — the pitch most comfortable for them. Every person who uses his or her voice frequently should attempt to determine the optimum pitch. Once it has been established, it is possible, with care, to train the voice to use a slightly lower habitual pitch without strain or discomfort.

The optimum pitch in most voices is about a quarter to a third of the way up from the lowest pitch possible. Most people tend to let the pitch rise as they get angry or excited and to lower as they become calm, serious, or sorrowful. Effective speakers try to widen the range of pitch available to them, both up and down, without straining the voice.

Exercise 13.2

Whichever vocal exercises you do, never strain your voice. Never push it to the point of discomfort; it is possible to damage your vocal chords.

1. Practise chanting in the highest pitch you are capable of and gradually lower the pitch as you chant, down to the lowest pitch you can hit. This exercise can relax the vocal chords while giving your pitch range a workout. Like a warm-up, it prepares the voice for other activity, whether further exercises or a newscast.
2. Find sad or serious material to read aloud. Make a conscious effort to lower the pitch of your voice without becoming breathy or throaty. Avoid any strain and remember that you must keep some range in reserve to emphasize certain words, so don't go so low that you can't increase the volume. Do this for several minutes each day, but never to the point of fatigue.

Remember that the organs that produce the voice are part of the body and are affected by the same things that affect all parts of the body. A person who is fit, healthy, relaxed, and confident will produce a much better performance physically, mentally, and vocally than one who is sick, out of shape, or under stress. The voice is affected, too, by the rest of the body. Warm-up exercises that relax the muscles of the neck and shoulders, jaw, and face will also relax the voice muscles and enhance vocal performance. Before a newscast or report, take a few seconds to tense the neck and shoulder muscles as much as you can and then relax them completely. Do this a couple of times. Make the most grotesque face you can imagine, using every possible facial muscle, hold it for a few seconds, and then relax the face totally. Use the breathing exercises outlined above. Finally, warm up

your pronunciation and enunciation muscles with the recitation of a tongue twister or two. Here are some favourites of newsrooms everywhere.
red leather, yellow leather

The Leith police dismisseth us.
strange strategic statistics
a twin-track tape recorder
truly rural Peggy Babcock

Concentration, Flubs, and Recovery

Again we must return to the word *credibility*. A newscaster must be authoritative, clear, and flawless. Anything less and the audience will lose respect for the reader and the content, and they will inevitably switch to someone who can deliver the news with credibility. To deliver the news flawlessly, a newscaster must concentrate all her or his skills and abilities. No distractions must be allowed to interfere; copy marking and rehearsal must be complete so that the copy is familiar and easy to read effectively; the voice must be tuned and confident. Is it possible to deliver a perfect newscast? When a veteran newsreader for the CBC retired a few years ago, his colleagues went back through the archives to find as many flubs and funny mistakes as they could to play back on his last day on the job. They found none — not one gaffe or mistake that was serious enough to be amusing in a career of almost 40 years. That was a very high level of professionalism.

However, we cannot all hope to go through our careers error-free. On occasion, we will make a slip — with luck, one that is not too serious. When this happens, a quick, smooth recovery will help to maintain credibility with the audience. *Never* stop and laugh or repeat the whole sentence or do anything that draws attention to the mistake. If you boot a word, simply repeat the word correctly and carry on. The worst thing you can do is let the mistake affect the rest of your newscast. Concentrate. Put the mistake behind you and zero in on the rest of the newscast to ensure that no other errors occur.

It is a good technique to practise recovering from a slip. Read a story aloud and deliberately make an error in pronunciation or a slip in diction. Practise quickly repeating the word correctly and then carrying on. If you do this as a regular part of your vocal practice, when you make a mistake you will recover gracefully and maintain your authority and credibility.

Assignment

The following exercises are designed to improve your voice. Some concentrate on relieving tension, others on warming up the vocal chords, and others on preparing the lips, jaw, tongue, and face for shaping sounds. In various combinations with the other exercises in this chapter, these routines might comprise the basis of a daily program. You should have two routines: one that lasts about five or ten minutes and is part of your daily practice (in combination with the assignment in Chapter 12), and one that is 30 to 60 seconds long that you can do just before going on air. Select which exercises work best for your physical and mental preparation, and make them part of your everyday workout.

1. Tension anywhere in the body (but especially in the neck and shoulder area) can transfer itself to your voice. This routine is designed to relax such tension. Imagine that each muscle in your body lights up when it is tense. Begin at your feet and work your way up to the top of your head, first making the light shine brightly in each muscle by tensing it and then putting the light out by relaxing it completely. Concentrate on the muscles in your chest, shoulders, neck, and face.

2. Close your eyes and concentrate on an image of calm and quiet. Focus on the sights, sounds, and smells of a peaceful garden, quiet stream, or calm lake. After a few minutes, slowly open your eyes and concentrate on breathing easily and deeply (without any strain) for five or six breaths. If you yawn, then you're doing it right.

3. Take a deep breath, consciously filling your lungs from the abdomen up into your chest, letting your rib cage expand. As you exhale, let the air activate your vocal chords in a sigh. Do this three times, concentrating on letting the sound be a part of your whole body — coming from your chest and head, even from your toes and legs, not just from your throat.

4. Become a marionette. Imagine yourself being held up by strings attached to the ceiling. First let the string holding your shoulders go slack and then tighten the string that holds your head up. Imagine that you are suspended only by the string in the top of your skull. Work on letting your jaw relax; let it fall open slightly as you relax the muscles completely. Your tongue, too, should relax, settling on the bottom of your mouth, and your throat should feel open. Breathe easily and naturally.

5. From the relaxed posture in Exercise 4, begin humming on the exhalation. For five or six breaths, just let the hum occur naturally on exhalation. Gradually increase the volume and duration of the hum, but never strain your voice. After a minute or so, begin forming a word out of the hum: "Hmmmmmmmmmaannnnyyy." Continue doing this, gradually, for several minutes, adding words to this alliterative rhyme.

Many marbles make Mo mumble.
Teetering Terry takes a tumble.
Howard holds his head how humble.
Still Stanley stands safe from stumble.

When you can easily and naturally deliver all four lines of the poem on a single exhalation, stop.

14

Station Style

There is a great deal of variation in the way news is delivered in radio and television stations across Canada. The broadcast media that we are exposed to from south of the border reveal an even greater variation. News must fit in with the overall sound of the station in radio and with the station image in TV. The sound or image is dictated by management and is based on the audience that is thought to tune in or on the audience that management wants to tune in. So a rock radio station that gears its music and advertising to 14- to 22-year-olds will have specific requirements of its news department. Content as well as delivery will be affected. Across the dial, another station wants 45- to 65-year–olds and has programming and commercials that are of interest to that age group. The news department must fit in with the requirements of that audience.

Television news is driven less by demographics and station image and more by the audience for news alone. In other words, few TV stations have a consistent daily audience the way radio stations do; programming is variable and tends to appeal across age and interest groups. Therefore, television newspeople may make independent decisions to target specific audiences with the delivery, content, and style of their news. The differences between stations are sometimes less obvious than in radio, but in a big market in which several stations compete each news department will try to attract a loyal audience by one means or another: fast pacing; "personal" journalism; a relaxed, informal style; investigative reporting; or lots of sports or entertainment.

The prime consideration in writing and delivering news that is intended to match a station's sound or image is the audience. Once the demographic is clearly understood and condensed into an image of the "typical" viewer or listener, it becomes much easier to write to and speak to that person. The station's audience may change over the day, depending on which programs are on and what people who listen to a newscast are doing. By thinking about the needs and desires of as specific an audience as possible, newswriters and newscasters can aim their style and content with precision. Surveys and polls are used to determine who is listening or watching at all times of the day. These tools are mostly used to make advertising more effective, but in a competent newsroom they can focus the newscast.

For want of more precise terms, let's break newscasts into three types: authoritative, informal, and personal/sensational. Of course, there are many variations across these arbitrary divisions, but by briefly examining each we should be able to demonstrate the spectrum of news styles. The objective here is to get you to understand that different news styles exist, that you may work at a station that has specific requirements about the way news is written and read, and to introduce a few of the techniques peculiar to each style.

Authoritative

This is news the BBC way. The CBC national news on both TV and radio also employs this style, though with less formality than the BBC. The attitude of the newswriters and newscasters seems to be "We don't care if this is interesting; it is what you need to know to be informed." Students listening to this style for the first time often find it far too long, too detailed, and numbingly boring. The writing often owes a great deal to newspaper style in both the detail of the content and the complexity of the writing. Naturally, some concessions are made to verbal delivery, but the overall impression is that you are listening to the unvarnished facts.

Because this is perceived as serious news for people who really want to know, stations that use it tend to promote their news as an important reason to listen to or watch the station. This is the news style of choice for most people who want or need (for business, political, or educational reasons) thorough information.

> The province has announced new measures to curb cigarette smuggling. Fines will be doubled for those caught transporting cigarettes across the border, and customs officials have been granted sweeping new powers of search and seizure. Illegal cigarette sales in Canada are said to represent a billion-dollar business, and the government is eager to regain the tax revenue lost when tobacco comes into the country illegally.

Informal

This is closest to the style we have been using in this book: conversational in tone, sufficiently detailed in content to provide information without overloading it, and with an emphasis on local events. Humour is not out of place but is used sparingly, colloquial language or even slang is occasionally employed, and stories are chosen for interest as well as information. The audience is assumed to be interested in what is going on but not interested in news for the sake of being informed. Stories are kept shorter, the language plainer and simpler, and the style of presentation more upbeat.

> Life has just become more difficult for tobacco smugglers. The province is doubling the fines for smuggling and giving customs officials new powers. It all adds up to a crackdown on the billion-dollar business in illegal cigarettes that bypasses government tax gatherers.

Personal/Sensational

Personal journalism is a style that relies on the personality of the reporter or newscaster to add interest to the news. Reports are frequently done live, on location; conversation and even kibitzing between news personnel are common; humour (including sarcasm) is encouraged; and stories are often light, fun, and lifestyle-oriented. The attitude seems to suggest that "We have to do a news show, but we'll make it as much like another entertainment program as we possibly can."

A few words of caution: first, too much editorial comment can get you into legal trouble; second, this style looks like fun, but it is not easy to do well. Remember that the laws of slander and contempt of court (see Unit Five) still apply to you, and the fact that you were trying to be funny is no defence. You must not cross the line to distort or make up news; the trick is to report the facts accurately and truthfully but to make the presentation personal. This is not a simple matter. When done poorly, it is embarrassingly awful. Beginning writers who are employed by a "personality" station are strongly advised to write their news straightforwardly and to add the clever bits sparingly to get the feel of what works and what does not.

> Bad news for a couple of guys in our newsroom who shall remain nameless. The Puritans at the provincial debating society have just made it even tougher to get cheap smokes. Fines for smuggling have been dou-

bled, and the goons at customs have been given all kinds of new powers. It seems the provincial bank account has been taking a beating, since smokers are unwilling to pay the exorbitant price for legal Rothmans and are buying the cheap smokes from over the border . . . brought in without a stop at the tax wicket. It all adds up to a billion-dollar industry, and the government wants to get its mitts on some of that cash. Anybody got a light?

Many newsrooms and individual news broadcasters retain in their private collections newscasts from the 1960s and 1970s that were famous for going "over the top." The CRTC clamped down on stations whose programming was aimed at teenagers but whose news talked of people being "strained through the grill" of a transport truck, being washed up as "floaters" after drowning, or being a "helpless moppet" subjected to "the twisted cravings of a knife-wielding pervert." Such blatantly offensive "news" is no longer on the air in Canada, but there are still stations that search hard to find an angle or a phrase that will shock listeners. Outrageously sensational newscasts are hard to do well consistently, and usually the attempt is made only by very creative and experienced writers. Their skills owe far more to creative copy writing than to journalism.

Exercise 14.1

Write three stories for each of the following sets of facts: one for an authoritative newsroom, one for an informal newsroom, and one for a personal/sensational newsroom. Choose your best stories from each style and record them. You will notice that vastly different delivery styles are required to make the scripts work on the air. You will also probably notice that your least effective story (because it is so difficult to do well and requires years of practice) is in the personal style.

1. • Mrs. Cathy Li and her husband, Paul, picked up a cheque for $5.8 million this morning when they presented the winning ticket in last week's Lotto 649 draw.
   • Mrs. Li bought the ticket the day before the draw at the NorthPark Mall (a local shopping centre).
   • They intend to put the money in the bank for now and decide what to do when the excitement wears off. One plan is to buy a house since they live in a small apartment now.
   • Mrs. Li works at a computer retail store as a repair technician. Paul Li lost his job as a lab assistant at a medical company two weeks ago.
   • They regularly buy lottery tickets but have never won more than $50 in the past.

2. • Two people were found dead from gunshot wounds in a suburban house at 4432 Oak Ave. late last night.

• Hailey Groton, 36, and his common-law spouse, Danielle Tracy, 29, had been dead for about 12 hours when they were found by police, who had been alerted by Ms. Tracy's co-workers, who were unable to contact her when she failed to show up for work.

• Police are treating the deaths as a murder-suicide. Both of the people were killed by a single gunshot to the head. A 7.62-millimetre hunting rifle was found at the scene.

• The couple had lived together for seven years, and neighbours described them as friendly and outgoing. Mr. Groton had been laid off from UniTech Steel Co. last month but had been applying for work. Ms. Tracy worked at a hairdressing establishment near her home.

3. • A local foodbank is about to run out of food unless generous city residents come forward.

• The Good Neighbour foodbank has been giving out canned and packaged food to needy city residents for almost four years. It gets the food from donations by individuals and from companies that dispose of surplus and out-of-date packaged food this way.

• Donations have declined steeply in the past months, and unless more food is found soon the foodbank will close its doors next weekend.

• According to spokesperson Vivian Trueman, there are more than 200 families who rely on the Good Neighbour for some or all of their food needs. She says that the donation centre will remain open, staffed by volunteers, 24 hours a day for the next week, in the hope that people will drop off non-perishable food items so that they can continue to help the poor people of the city.

Assignment

In a group of four, monitor the radio stations in your area and choose the four with the widest spectrum of news styles. Agree on a day and time to record newscasts from each of the stations simultaneously. As a group, play back each newscast, noting differences in content, lineup, and delivery. Which of these three factors (content, lineup, and delivery) makes the most difference to the style of the broadcast? Do the newscasts reflect the sounds, styles, and demographics of the stations? Do these four newscasts cover the full spectrum of styles?

Unit Four
Review Exercises

Here are three more stories that you can use to practise checking, copy marking, and reading with correct pronunciation, appropriate emphasis, and proper pacing. Record your delivery and time each story. Are your "seconds per line" fairly consistent?

1. A train derailment north of the city is being blamed on three mischievous children. According to authorities, the two girls and a boy, aged 9 and 10, were playing with an automatic switcher on the C-N-R line this afternoon and managed to break one of the locks. They then somehow jammed the switch open, causing an east-bound freight to jump the rails at just past 7 this evening. C-N-R Police spokesperson, Lieutenant David del'Angelo, says the children were brought in by their parents after admitting to the sabbotage. No one was hurt, and it's expected the tracks will be clear by morning. So far, there's no estimate of what the prank will cost.

2. The arctic high-pressure ridge that has made our climatic conditions so unseasonably wintry is gradually moving east tonight. In its place a low-pressure zone will move in, and we're probably in for six to ten centimetres of snow tomorrow, but that's the good news. A warming trend could bring ice pellets and freezing rain by tomorrow evening, and all that snow might be slush by Thursday morning. Spring, according to all the rumours, is just around the corner, though, so don't despair.

3. An indictment against alocal politician has been thrown out of court. Kevin Draney was charged with trafficking in restricted drugs after sevral athletes at Vincent Massey High School, where he teaches, complained of being offered steroids and other prescription drugs. Investigations by

city and provincial police lead to the charges adn Draney's suspension from teaching. Now the charges have been dropped for lack of evidence, and Draney is expected to be re-instated at the school. During the investigation, he continued to serve on city council as the councillor for Ward Six.

Review 4.2

Rewrite these stories for a personality-style station that emphasizes short (no more than 15-second), sensational stories. Record your rewrite with an appropriate delivery style.

Assignment

In monitoring newscasts (Unit Two Review Assignment), begin noting the style of newscasts at each station and the differences in style from station to station. Try to label each station's news according to the three broad types given in this unit, and begin noting other differences between the styles including the following characteristics:

- length of each story
- commercial interruptions (where, how many, and type of ad)
- length and style of sportscast (if any)
- style of weather forecast
- type of music that follows the news (Many stations have policies governing which types of songs follow newscasts.)
- on-air interaction between news and announcing staff
- style of station ID before, during, or after the news

UNIT 5

Journalism and Society

15

The Law

What follows is a summary of Canadian law as it applies to journalists. The main things you need to know are here, but situations will arise in your career that will require you to have more information and a precise legal interpretation. Large stations and networks retain legal counsel who can be called in when serious legal questions come up, but every newsroom and journalism school should have a set of five little books called *Law and the Media*, published by the Canadian Bar Foundation in Ottawa. These books are pricey, so individual reporters might not want to obtain a set, but every journalist should consider getting the one entitled *Journalists and the Law: How to Get the Story without Getting Sued or Put in Jail*. The title says it all.

There is a myth that reporters and journalists have privileges and rights that other citizens do not enjoy. This is untrue. The laws regarding trespass, invasion of privacy, contempt of court, defamation, and so on apply to everyone — including reporters.

One other word of caution: do not use American courtroom drama or news magazine shows as a basis for your knowledge of the law. U.S. law differs considerably from Canadian law, and what is permitted in the United States, in some instances, will land you in very hot water in Canada. For example, while jurors may be interviewed following a trial in the States (and have been on national media after sensational trials), in Canada jurors may not discuss their deliberations and can go to jail for doing so; reporters who urge them to divulge this restricted information can also be prosecuted. Other differences will be noted as they come up. Also, keep in mind that, while criminal proceedings are the same across Canada, civil law in Quebec is different from that used by other provinces. It is based on the Napoleonic Code, whereas the other provinces follow English Common Law. There are some significant differences between them, and if you are working in Quebec you would do well to become familiar with the rules as they apply there.

Defamation

Defamation is, at its simplest, saying or writing something about someone that discredits that person. More formally, it is a communication that may tend to lower a person in the estimation of right-thinking members of society generally; to cut that person off from society; or to expose that person to hatred, contempt, or ridicule. A broadcaster who repeats a defamatory remark made by someone else is liable, and so is anyone else connected with and responsible for the broadcast of the defamatory statement, including an editor, camera person, news director, even the station owner.

There are two words associated with defamation: *libel* and *slander*. At one time, it was thought that libel was written defamation and that slander was spoken or broadcast defamation. Now the definition says that libel is defamation in print or broadcast, while slander is reserved for conversation. So what we are concerned with as broadcast journalists is libel.

To say that someone is a liar, a cheat, a pervert, or a crook is clearly libel. To say that someone defrauded her clients, or accepted bribes, or abused her children is also libel. On the other hand, it is probably not libel to say that because of a teacher's mistake you failed your year, since you are not saying the teacher is incompetent. It is not libel if you say something that affects a group that is so large that individual members cannot be hurt by the statement; however, the Edmonton police force of about 1,000 people won a defamation case because the judge thought that its members were identifiable in the community and could therefore be hurt by the libel.

The amount of money awarded in a defamation suit depends on two factors. One is damages the defamation caused. Damages taken into account might include loss of job, loss of clients, alienation of friends or associates, and so on. The second is punishment of the defamer, known as punitive damages.

To understand the rules of libel better, it is necessary to discuss the defences against a libel accusation. Once you understand what is not libel, you will have a much better grasp of what you may say and what you may not say.

TRUTH

If you can prove in court that what you said is true, then you cannot be found guilty of libel. Yet it is sometimes very difficult and costly to prove the truth of an accusatory statement, especially if you are repeating a libel made by someone else. Here's another instance of U.S. law being different from Canadian law: in the United States, it is a defence against a libel charge to say that you honestly believed that what you said was true. In Canada, the statement must actually be true for you to be innocent of defamation. After all, an innocent person's reputation was damaged by an untrue statement, whether you thought it was true or not.

FAIR COMMENT

To encourage the exchange of views and opinions, this defence permits a defamatory statement if it is in the context of the broadcaster's *opinion* and is presented in such a way that the listener or viewer can make up his or her own mind about it. To be successful, this defence must prove several things: the comment must be "fair," an opinion that could honestly be held by a reasonable person; it must be clearly labelled "opinion" or "comment" in the broadcast and not able to be mistaken for a statement of fact (in other words, it must be separated from a straight newscast); it must be based on provable facts that are part of the story or well known; and it must be about a matter that is of interest to the public (not a private matter that is insignificant to your audience). This defence is available most often for those who make editorial comments or whose program is a forum for opinions.

Let's say that you discover the mayor has been accepting campaign contributions in exchange for favours. In an editorial, you say that the mayor is a scoundrel, a crooked politician, and that he should resign. If you were wrong about the campaign contributions, then you could be successfully sued. But if the mayor was indeed doing what you said, then you might reasonably hold your stated opinion and probably not be guilty of libel.

CONSENT

If the person who brings the defamation charge to court can be proven to have agreed to publication of the material, then the person who publicized it cannot be convicted. Consent does not have to be written but can be implied from the plaintiff's willing participation in the conversation or interview that led to broadcast of the defamatory material.

ABSOLUTE PRIVILEGE

A statement that is untrue and libellous may be broadcast as long as it is quoted from publicly available records "without malice" (the reporter and station have no hidden reason for wanting to damage or ridicule the plaintiff). Extracts from parliamentary proceedings, the records of the legislature, open courts, meetings of school boards or labour relations boards, in fact any meetings held for the discussion of matters of public concern, are publishable even if they contain defamatory material. However, if libellous statements are made outside the actual meeting or assembly (e.g., as part of an interview in the hallway during a break in the meeting), absolute privilege does not apply.

One last word about defamation: an apology or retraction is not a defence. Such an apology would be taken into consideration when damages are being assessed, but it would have no influence on the outcome of a trial for defamation.

Contempt of Court

Our justice system is such a vital part of our democracy that laws have been enacted to protect it from disrespect or interference with its impartial and proper conduct. We therefore have laws against disrupting a trial, questioning the impartiality of a judge, disobeying any order of the court, or prejudicing the outcome of a trial. It is up to the judge to decide if someone is in contempt of court and to impose the penalty, which may be a fine, imprisonment, or both.

UNDUE CRITICISM OF A JUDGE

Judges are so important to the administration of our justice system that they are protected from the sort of criticism that other members of society have to endure. Besides, judges, to maintain their impartiality, may not speak about their cases in public, so they are prevented from defending themselves against such criticism. There are several famous cases in Canada in which journalists have been brought to trial for this offence. These cases suggest that you may not say that a judge is biased or corrupt or that he or she has motives other than the fair administration of the law. Within limits, you can make fun of the court or suggest that a decision was wrong, as long as you steer clear of suggesting that the judge was malicious or unfair. It is unlikely that beginning reporters will have to worry about this law; normally, it is columnists and outspoken editorialists who may need legal opinion before unduly criticizing a judge.

PREJUDICING THE OUTCOME OF A TRIAL

There are several considerations here. First, as already mentioned, a reporter may not suggest that someone is guilty of a crime before that per-

son is found guilty in court. While it is permissible to give the facts and cir-
cumstances of a crime, you must stop short of saying who committed the
crime. "Witnesses told police that a tall blonde woman fired two shots at
Smith. Arrested at the scene was Jane Doe" stops short of naming Doe as
the shooter.

Second, a reporter may not reveal that an accused person has a criminal
record until that fact is revealed in court. The principle is that of fair trial; a
person must be tried only on the charge at hand. If jurors know the accused
has a criminal past, then they might be influenced sufficiently to convict that
person without impartial consideration of evidence in the current case. A
judge must rule on whether prior convictions are admissible evidence, and
they must not appear in print or broadcast before that ruling. Similarly, it may
be contempt of court to broadcast other information that might cause jury
members to make up their minds before hearing all the evidence. Allegations
about an accused person's character given by friends or neighbours, or a history of scrapes with the law, or implications based on the actions of friends,
relatives, or associates could prejudice the jury, and the reporter who broadcasts them could be in contempt of court.

Third, it is illegal to broadcast the amount being sought in a civil proceeding if that information is not made public in court. The jury is not supposed
to know how much money is at stake because such knowledge might cause
jurors to make a decision based on it rather than solely on the evidence.

DISOBEYING A COURT ORDER

There are two important considerations here: withholding information the
court requests and broadcasting information the court says you can't publicize. The first has occurred several times in Canada. A reporter has
obtained information from a source who wants to remain anonymous. The
court needs to know who has provided the information in order to give
someone a fair trial or to determine the validity of evidence. Reporters who
refuse to give the names of their contacts when told to do so by the court
can be found in contempt. This is a tough issue, because reporters naturally don't want to be known to go back on their word and don't want to get
their sources in trouble. For one thing, doing so can impair their ability to
get such information again; for another, it is unethical to make a promise
of anonymity and then renege on it. However, the penalty for such a stand
can be severe.

For several good reasons, a court may forbid publication of proceedings.
It may do so to protect the reputation of the victim or a witness in criminal cases or to ensure that a person involved in the crime who hasn't yet
come to trial gets a fair hearing before an impartial jury. Whatever the rea-

son, as long as a court order forbidding publication stands, anyone who disobeys that order is likely to be hit with contempt of court. Such gag orders are often fought in court by news organizations, and it is best left up to them and their lawyers to establish what can and cannot be published rather than take it upon yourself to defend freedom of the press by broadcasting forbidden material.

JUVENILES

Under the Young Offenders Act, a person between the ages of 12 and 18 charged under the Criminal Code may not be identified in the media. Pending legislation, the Youth Criminal Justice Act may change the age limits, but the principle of letting a young person's mistakes be forgiven and forgotten by society remains the same. In addition, it is at the discretion of the judge to bar publication of any names in a trial when publication would injure a young person, whether the accused, a victim, or a witness. This is why in child abuse and other such cases the media are frequently barred from revealing the identity of the accused person; to do so would also reveal the identity of a young person involved.

Privacy and Trespass

Reporters have no right to be anywhere that any other citizen cannot be. The laws of trespass say that a person who owns or has charge of a property has the right to order anyone off that property. This includes places that might normally be thought of as public, such as government buildings, stadiums, shopping centres, even sidewalks and roadways. A person in possession of the property may arrest a trespasser or use whatever force is reasonable and necessary to remove the trespasser, and a trespasser who resists can be charged with assault. The law, however, does not include in "reasonable force" the damaging or taking of recording equipment.

Some provinces have specific laws that allow people to sue if they believe their privacy has been violated or to get an injunction to stop publication of information. Defences against these laws are very similar to those for defamation. However, the laws of trespass and other property laws as well as the defamation laws cover many instances of unwanted intrusion. If there really is a story to be told (i.e., it is in the public interest to know), then, in most cases, an individual cannot prevent his or her picture and name from being used in the media.

CONFIDENTIALITY AND OFF-THE-RECORD INFORMATION

There is no law that covers off-the-record information or a source's wish to remain anonymous. When people tell you that the information they give you is off the record, they mean they don't want it published. You can use it as background or source material, but they don't want it released to the public. You can do one of three things: agree to the condition, agree to the condition and broadcast the information anyway, or refuse to agree to the condition. As you can see, the issue really is one of ethics, not legality. If you choose the second option, you are being dishonest and unethical and will probably lose a potential source of more information. But you are not breaking any law.

Another serious problem with confidential or off-the-record information is its accuracy. Can you be sure that what you have been told by someone who won't let his or her name be used is true? The only way to protect yourself is to use the information as a beginning point for your research and to confirm its accuracy yourself from independent sources — which is what the source wanted in the first place.

TELEPHONE RECORDINGS

Telephone recordings of interviews or conversations may legally be made without the consent of the person being taped. The law says that one person in the conversation (presumably the reporter) must give permission for the taping. However, CRTC regulations forbid any interview or conversation from being *broadcast* without the permission of the person being interviewed. So any interview can be taped, the information used in a story, and the tape kept to ensure accuracy of what was said. But if you want to broadcast the interview or any part of it, you must have the permission of the person being interviewed.

16

Ethics

Ethics is the study of moral principles. While ethics concerns right and wrong, we think of it mostly in terms of moral rather than legal principles. In other words, it has to do with our *sense* of what is right behaviour and what is wrong behaviour. In our society, it is unethical to cheat, to lie, or to hurt someone's feelings, but there are no laws against these behaviours. It is both unethical and illegal to steal or damage someone's property or to assault a person. You develop your set of moral guidelines from your upbringing, culture, religion, education, society, and so on. Many professions also have sets of ethical guidelines or principles that govern the behaviour of their members.

Journalists, more than most other professionals, are faced with troubling ethical decisions as part of their job. Other professionals, such as lawyers, doctors, and some teachers, have associations that certify their members and enforce codes of ethics. Such ethical guidelines are stringent, for a member can be decertified for violations. Journalists have no such governing body, but several news organizations have published codes of journalistic ethics. While these codes are unenforceable, they provide clear visions of which issues concern journalists and how thoughtful organizations recommend journalists conduct themselves.

RTNDA Code of Ethics

The Radio-Television News Directors Association (RTNDA) is the world's largest professional organization devoted exclusively to electronic journalism, representing news organizations from more than 30 countries.

The RTNDA Code of Ethics and Professional Conduct is a statement of guiding principles for the practice of electronic journalism. It cannot anticipate every situation electronic journalists might face. Common sense and careful judgement should be applied in all cases.

CODE OF ETHICS AND PROFESSIONAL CONDUCT OF THE RADIO-TELEVISION NEWS DIRECTORS ASSOCIATION

The Radio-Television News Directors Association, wishing to foster the highest professional standards of electronic journalism, promote public understanding of and confidence in electronic journalism, and strengthen principles of journalistic freedom to gather and disseminate information, establishes this Code of Ethics and Professional Conduct.

PREAMBLE: Professional electronic journalists should operate as trustees of the public, seek the truth, report it fairly and with integrity and independence, and stand accountable for their actions.

PUBLIC TRUST: Professional electronic journalists should recognize that their first obligation is to the public.

Professional electronic journalists should:

- Understand that any commitment other than service to the public undermines trust and credibility.
- Recognize that service in the public interest creates an obligation to reflect the diversity of the community and guard against oversimplification of issues or events.
- Provide a full range of information to enable the public to make enlightened decisions.
- Fight to ensure that the public's business is conducted in public.

TRUTH: Professional electronic journalists should pursue truth aggressively and present the news accurately, in context, and as completely as possible.

Professional electronic journalists should:

- Continuously seek the truth.
- Resist distortions that obscure the importance of events.
- Clearly disclose the origin of information and label all material provided by outsiders.

Professional electronic journalists should not:

- Report anything known to be false.
- Manipulate images or sounds in any way that is misleading.

- Plagiarize.
- Present images or sounds that are reenacted without informing the public.

FAIRNESS: Professional electronic journalists should present the news fairly and impartially, placing primary value on significance and relevance.

Professional electronic journalists should:

- Treat all subjects of news coverage with respect and dignity, showing particular compassion to victims of crime or tragedy.
- Exercise special care when children are involved in a story and give children greater privacy protection than adults.
- Seek to understand the diversity of their community and inform the public without bias or stereotype.
- Present a diversity of expressions, opinions, and ideas in context.
- Present analytical reporting based on professional perspective, not personal bias.
- Respect the right to a fair trial.

INTEGRITY: Professional electronic journalists should present the news with integrity and decency, avoiding real or perceived conflicts of interest, and respect the dignity and intelligence of the audience as well as the subjects of news.

Professional electronic journalists should:

- Identify sources whenever possible. Confidential sources should be used only when it is clearly in the public interest to gather or convey important information or when a person providing information might be harmed. Journalists should keep all commitments to protect a confidential source.
- Clearly label opinion and commentary.
- Guard against extended coverage of events or individuals that fails to significantly advance a story, place the event in context, or add to the public knowledge.
- Refrain from contacting participants in violent situations while the situation is in progress.
- Use technological tools with skill and thoughtfulness, avoiding techniques that skew facts, distort reality, or sensationalize events.
- Use surreptitious newsgathering techniques, including hidden cameras or microphones, only if there is no other way to obtain stories of significant public importance and only if the technique is explained to the audience.
- Disseminate the private transmissions of other news organizations only with permission.

Professional electronic journalists should not:

- Pay news sources who have a vested interest in a story.
- Accept gifts, favors, or compensation from those who might seek to influence coverage.
- Engage in activities that may compromise their integrity or independence.

INDEPENDENCE: Professional electronic journalists should defend the independence of all journalists from those seeking influence or control over news content.

Professional electronic journalists should:

- Gather and report news without fear or favor, and vigorously resist undue influence from any outside forces, including advertisers, sources, story subjects, powerful individuals, and special interest groups.
- Resist those who would seek to buy or politically influence news content or who would seek to intimidate those who gather and disseminate the news.
- Determine news content solely through editorial judgment and not as the result of outside influence.
- Resist any self-interest or peer pressure that might erode journalistic duty and service to the public.
- Recognize that sponsorship of the news will not be used in any way to determine, restrict, or manipulate content.
- Refuse to allow the interests of ownership or management to influence news judgment and content inappropriately.
- Defend the rights of the free press for all journalists, recognizing that any professional or government licensing of journalists is a violation of that freedom.

ACCOUNTABILITY: Professional electronic journalists should recognize that they are accountable for their actions to the public, the profession and themselves.

Professional electronic journalists should:

- Actively encourage adherence to these standards by all journalists and their employers.
- Respond to public concerns. Investigate complaints and correct errors promptly and with as much prominence as the original report.
- Explain journalistic processes to the public, especially when practices spark questions or controversy.
- Recognize that professional electronic journalists are duty-bound to conduct themselves ethically.

- Refrain from ordering or encouraging courses of action, that would force employees to commit an unethical act.
- Carefully listen to employees who raise ethical objections and create environments in which such objections and discussions are encouraged.
- Seek support for and provide opportunities to train employees in ethical decision-making.

In meeting its responsibility to the profession of electronic journalism, RTNDA has created this code to identify important issues, to serve as a guide for its members, to facilitate self-scrutiny, and to shape future debate.

Source: "RTNDA Code of Ethics," September 14, 2000. Reprinted with permission.

These resolutions are laudable goals for all journalists, but are they observed? Is there any doubt that news organizations, driven by competition and the need for audience share, pay only lip service to such ethical niceties? Let's look at a couple of the more contentious issues in the field of journalistic ethics and raise some questions for consideration.

The Myth of Objectivity

While all journalists claim to be objective, it is not difficult to find examples in which this claim is pretty thin. The largest newspapers in the country, for example, take pride in their political stands, and in their news coverage they echo those stands. *The National Post* makes no apology for taking a conservative stance on issues, and that point of view is reflected in what it covers, the priority it gives to respective stories, and the way in which it presents events. Similarly, the country's largest-circulation daily, *The Toronto Star*, takes a liberal slant on its editorial page and in its coverage of events.

All reporters, editors, and news directors have viewpoints — social, political, philosophical, and so on. Some deliberately present the news in ways that reflect those viewpoints, while others try to be impartial and suppress their opinions as they write and deliver their newscasts. However, even those who attempt to be objective have a tough time. We all see things differently, and, as objective as we try to be, our reports are shaped by who we are and what we feel. Here's an example of how difficult the goal of true objectivity can be.

Two reporters covering a demonstration outside an abortion clinic may see the same events but will honestly report different versions of the story.

While one sees a group of well-meaning, moral people trying to stop a horrible practice and being roughed up by police, the other sees a fanatic rabble trying to disrupt a legal medical practice and attacking police officers. The interviews selected for broadcast, the sound bites, video clips, words, descriptions, camera angles, even the tone of voice will support the version that each reporter *actually saw*. Who is right? What will their respective audiences think after seeing or hearing their reports?

The Pressure for Sensationalism

"Programming such as news, music, dramas, sports events, and sitcoms is what goes on the air between commercials." This cynical view suggests that, in commercial radio and television, the whole purpose of the organization is to sell air time and that the programming is just a way of getting people to stay tuned for the commercials. Money drives the media. That is why there is intense pressure on newsrooms to go for high ratings in any way possible. To some, this means clear, responsible, complete, straightforward newscasts that attract listeners or viewers. To others, it means playing up the murders, mayhem, muggings, and movie stars in order to attract (or at least not alienate) an audience whose primary interest is not serious news.

The drive toward sensationalism is irresistible. It is just a question of degree: to what extent does the newsroom adopt entertainment value in presenting its news?

Conflict of Interest

Because journalists are assumed to be impartial and unbiased, there can be a problem with news personnel having too close a relationship with an advertiser or newsmaker. Can a newscaster be trusted to treat a story about a major advertiser the same as any other story? The very nature of private radio and television, relying as they do on advertising dollars for their existence, makes them vulnerable to the charge of conflict of interest, real or perceived. Many reporters have close ties to the people they cover. Parliamentary reporters routinely see politicians socially and use those social contacts for tips, leads, and confirmation of information. Sports reporters are often friends with the people they report on, and many are former athletes themselves. Can these reporters be relied upon to present to their audiences unbiased factual information, or will their associations with the newsmakers colour their coverage?

Sometimes the concern over conflict of interest presents a real dilemma. For instance, a television crew covering a controversial wolf hunt in northern Canada was offered free helicopter transportation to observe the snowmobile-equipped hunters in action. But the helicopter was leased by a group protesting the hunt. If the crew accepted the offer, there would be a clear conflict of interest: should the report in any way be critical of the hunt, it would be easy to assume that the reporter had been bought. But leasing a helicopter was an expensive proposition, beyond the resources of the crew's news organization, and if the crew didn't accept the free ride their coverage of the hunt would have been very weak. What should they have done?

The Right to Privacy

While every public opinion survey reveals that newspaper readers are sickened by the actions of the paparazzi with their long-range camera lenses focussed on every step of celebrities such as the British royal family, newspapers that publish photos taken by the paparazzi sell out. Does a person who, for whatever reason, is interesting to the public have any right to privacy? Some reporters have made careers out of digging up the past indiscretions of politicians, especially in the United States. Do the love affairs and dope smoking that took place 30 years ago have any relevance today? Several politicians have had their careers ruined by these revelations, and others have been forced to divert their energies away from issues and policies to deal with such disclosures. Publication of private or confidential material does seem to have importance to the public.

But do all newsmakers deserve such scrutiny? The tearful faces of relatives at a funeral, the agony of an accident victim, the pain on the faces of an elderly couple watching their house burn down, or the shocked and grieving parents of a murdered child: these are newsmakers too. Many news organizations and individual journalists would defend broadcast of such images as a necessary part of covering the news. Audiences have a right to know, and reporters have a duty to tell them. Others would turn the cameras and microphones away to allow such people their privacy, but by doing so they deprive their audiences of compelling images.

17

Issues in Canadian News Broadcasting

The following are opinions and viewpoints from a wide variety of sources on the subject of news broadcasting in Canada. Some are provocative and worthy of discussion (perhaps even argument); others are reminders to all of us about some of the power and importance of our profession; still others are telling comments or anecdotes that pertain to broadcast journalism. The aim of this chapter is to stimulate thought about some of the wider issues that concern us, apart from the day-to-day business of producing a newscast from the raw material of life that comes across our desks.

The first two articles deal with an incident that happened on CTV's 24-hour news channel, Newsnet, early in 2000. Avery Haines, a veteran of Toronto radio news but new to CTV, stuttered on air while delivering a newscast. Knowing there would be a second take of her newscast, she made some joking comments about her slip (outlined in the first article below). Confusion during playback resulted in the wrong take being aired, and Haines's comments after her on-air mistake were broadcast. Following a very public discussion, she was fired by CTV and subsequently hired by CityTV in Toronto.

WHAT WAS AVERY HAINES' REAL SIN?

Now that Avery Haines once again has a more-or-less honest job in TV, it's time to draw a couple of conclusions and wave goodbye.

First: She's better off. Reading the news on a 24-hour television network news wheel is like striking poses in front of a new car at a trade show. The wardrobe is nice, but the work is stupid.

Second: CTV is worse off.

Let's go back to what she said, where she said it and why, a little riff on a blown intro as she backed up to try it again: "I kind of like the little stutter thing. We've got a stuttering newscaster, we've got the black, we've got the Asian, we've got the woman, I could be a lesbian, folk-dancing, black woman stutterer . . . in a wheelchair, with a gimping, rubber leg. I'd have a successful career, let me tell you."

Now, what was this? An expression of racism? Against lesbians, blacks, folk-dancers, the disabled? Wouldn't that have sounded something like — damn those black, lesbian, disabled folk-dancers?

Oh, but it's the implication. Of what? Of the suspicion that a black, lesbian, disabled folk dancer might just have an edge in the television job market these days.

Well, she might have. In fact, she would have. That's the point: All things being even approximately equal, minority or disadvantaged job candidates get the edge. I believe that may be CTV's policy. And as many times as I read Haines's little joke — and that's what it was, really, a little joke, as little as a joke could be, a private, almost microscopic joke — I can't find in it any indication that she thinks that policy is wrong.

Well, maybe that's the trouble. As a female, she may have had the benefit of the policy; she certainly hadn't been harmed by it. But she was poking fun at the policy. That's what she's guilty of — not racism, not rebellion, but poking fun at a corporate and government policy.

No, hang on. Isn't that what the people at *Double Exposure* do on CTV every week? Now we have it. Haines was caught on television poking fun at a corporate and government policy without a licence.

Boy, as crimes go, you can't get more Canadian than that.

This is not to say that CTV doesn't have a problem with race in its newscasting. All television does; it's the nature of the medium.

Television broadcasters, whatever their race, all seem to come out of the same factory. They dress the same, comb their hair the same, use the same accent. There are exceptions: Jack Webster, now dead; Joe Schlesinger, now semi-retired; and a bunch of people in sports. But, in general, broadcasters are presented as the mainstream ideal no matter what their race is.

Artists and writers and performers have managed to create work in Canada that expresses their cultural heritage. News broadcasters, whatever their race, have to look and sound like bank managers. (The news they deliver is usually written from the world view of a bank manager and that may help.) . . .

When I first heard about what happened to Haines, I called her and welcomed her to the great club of people who have said something stupid on camera. Most of us actually meant to say the things we said, and only realized later how stupid they were. Perhaps the people CTV really ought to be targetting are the people who say stupid things on television on purpose. Say, Jane Stewart. Or the televangelists. Or the people who sell bake-in-your-oven pizza.

"You're a collective insult to the country! You're crass! You're destructive! Off the air! You're fired!"

Tape at eleven.

Source: Bill Cameron, "What Was Avery Haines' Real Sin?" *The Toronto Star,* February 16, 2000, p. A21.

JOURNALISTS DON'T GET IT ON DIVERSITY: HAINES' REMARKS REFLECTION OF TODAY'S MEDIA ENVIRONMENT

Watch closely. That rumbling noise and cloud of dust on the horizon indicate the wagons are being circled by the news media around former CTV Newsnet anchor Avery Haines.

This shouldn't come as a surprise. We in the media, like the police, are quick to move in when we believe one of our own is being threatened by outsiders. Even if that defence is less than righteous.

By now Haines' on-air gaffe has reached near apocryphal status. Who knows, it may become required reading for all broadcast journalism students in the future.

I don't believe Avery Haines is a racist, sexist homophobe. I do believe she is naive and ignorant of the harm comments such as this can have on some of her colleagues working in the news media.

Rather than being a reflection of her character, I believe her remarks are a reflection of the environment in which she and I work.

When I first heard about the incident, I wasn't surprised. I've been a journalist in newspaper and television for 23 years and I've heard similar comments before from my colleagues.

There are two components to Haines' remarks:

First there is the traditional newsroom humour, the so-called "gallows humour," that often reeks of bad taste. For example, people killed in house fires are sometimes referred to as "crispy critters."

The second is a derisive attitude in newsrooms toward diversity and employment equity.

What was surprising was how quickly CTV moved to fire Haines. Of course, it may have had a lot to do with the fact that Haines was in the middle of her probation. She had been with the network for only two months. It was an easy call for CTV's senior vice president Henry Kowalski. One can only wonder what Kowalski would have done if Haines had been a long-time employee.

This isn't the first time that an on-air personality's private comments have been inadvertently made public. In 1983, veteran broadcaster Phil

MacKellar shocked his radio audience on the day of the Caribana parade. MacKellar was having a private telephone conversation from the announcer's booth with a friend.

Not realizing the broadcast button was switched on, listeners heard MacKellar refuse to join his friend downtown because there were "four million niggers" on the streets.

A storm of protest from a cross-section of Torontonians followed. Three weeks later, MacKellar was relieved of his announcing duties. In the case of the Haines affair, the storm of protest appears to be coming from within the profession, from journalists (mostly white) defending her actions. There have been few, if any, public comments from minority journalists. Likely because they don't want to become targets in their news organizations.

Any mention of the need for the media being more diverse and reflective of the reality of Canada today is often met with lip service or even derision within the industry. Many in the media resent any observation that the profession is primarily lily-white, at times insensitive, or out of touch with a vast number of Canadians who are not white. We do stories about under-representation of minorities in fire departments and police forces. We rarely put our own profession under similar scrutiny.

One of the greatest fears of most non-white journalists is for their white colleagues to think they got the job because of their ethnicity, or the colour of their skin.

I have been on the receiving end of this thinking. At the height of severe budget cutbacks at the CBC in the early 1990s, a white co-worker tried to reassure me that I was "safe" from any downsizing because I was "the right colour." I sat down with him and we examined the statistics. It didn't take him long to concede that his comment was not based on reality.

If my co-worker's thinking and Avery Haines' perception are to be believed, there should be numerous minorities and people with obvious disabilities on Canadian television. We all know that is not the case.

Minority journalists know there are two groups in this business — "us" and "them." They also know that there are different rules for each. An outspoken white reporter is "aggressive" and "has edge." A non-white reporter with similar traits "has a chip" on his or her shoulder.

Of the few minorities in the mainstream media, some of us fight back, sometimes to the detriment of our careers. Others acquiesce. They go along to get along.

This issue is not about hair and teeth, as a columnist at another newspaper has said in an effort to trivialize the matter. Nor is it just about newsroom humour.

It's about a deep-seated attitude in the media toward diversity in a profession that professes to serve all Canadians.

It's clear many people in the news media don't get it. Certainly Avery Haines doesn't get it. In a parting shot, she has been quoted as saying: "It's only f — ing television."

Haines says she doesn't want to be a "poster girl" for those opposed to fair employment practices for women and minorities. I'm afraid she already is. She has become a cause célèbre for those in our profession who refuse to see society around them and refuse to get it.

Source: Hamlin Grange, "Journalists Don't Get It on Diversity: Haines' Remarks Reflection of Today's Media Environment," *The Toronto Star,* January 28, 2000, p. A23. Hamlin Grange is president of the Canadian Association of Black Journalists.

A PERSONAL CONCLUSION

Whenever I am tempted to be pessimistic about the progress of Canadian journalism, I compare the students in our graduate school at Western with the odds-and-ends who fell into newspaper offices about the time that I entered journalism. There were a few talented ones among us, of course, but as a group we simply did not compare with the young journalists of today. Not only are they better educated, in a formal sense, but they have a much clearer understanding of the world and a more realistic grasp of the possibilities open to them. They also have, in addition to their share of talent, their own brand of idealism. These young journalists represent, over the long run and despite many individual setbacks, an irresistible force for the continued improvement of Canadian journalism.

Whether the journalistic institutions of Canada have kept pace with our national development and with the expectations and abilities of a new generation of journalists is an important question. Journalists of my generation would of course answer no, essentially because there are still too many news organizations that view the bottom line in strictly financial terms, rather than as an intelligently defined balance of financial and editorial considerations. Nonetheless, in recent decades, the notion of news-media accountability has made more progress in Canada than in most other countries. Press councils and media ombudsmen have become accepted elements of our media structures. These institutions help to develop and perpetuate, in the minds of both journalists and media owners, a sense of responsibility toward the news audience and society as a whole. . . .

Equally important . . . is the development of a higher degree of "media literacy" among consumers of news, starting with a recognition by our schools that knowing how to "read" electronic and print news media with some degree of sophistication is as vital as having a basic knowledge of our political structures.

Education, systems of accountability, vast media empires employing thousands of people — all these, in the long run, are there to nurture, support, and disseminate the creative energy of gifted journalists. We often tend to forget this amid all the paraphernalia of modern journalism. Without that fire at the centre of the process, everything else would be useless.

Source: Peter Desbarats, *Guide to Canadian News Media,* 2nd ed., Harcourt Canada, 1996, pp. 266–67.

JOURNALISTS CRITICAL OF MEDIA TOO

Ask journalists about their profession and they will tell you bad news: Reporting has gotten sloppier, facts too often are blurred by opinion and efforts to inform and entertain has [sic] led to a kind of "infotainment."

The Pew Center for the People and the Press turned the tables on the media, surveying 552 national and local journalists and news executives in print, television, radio and the Internet about the state of American journalism.

. . . A rising number of journalists agree with public opinion polls that say the media lack credibility. They also say reporters drive controversies with their coverage of personal and ethical behaviors of public figures. . . .

When asked to cite top problems facing journalism, half the national news professionals mentioned such things as sensationalism, a lack of objectivity and inaccurate reporting. About 40 percent cited too much emphasis on the bottom line, competition and declining audience and readership.

The news media's loss of credibility with the public was cited by about one-third of the respondents. But while it ranked third — behind quality and standards and business pressures — concern about credibility has nearly doubled during the past decade. . . .

Some other survey findings:

• 69 percent of national news professionals said the distinction between reporting and commentary had seriously eroded. . . .

• 40 percent said news reports are increasingly full of factual errors and sloppy reporting. . . .

• 49 percent of the national news media professionals say the press drives controversies with its coverage of the personal and ethical behaviors of public figures. . . .

- Two-thirds. . . . say attempts to attract readers or viewers push the industry too far in the direction of infotainment.

Source: Deb Riechmann, excerpted from The Associated Press, March 31, 1999; downloaded from *http://www.canoe.ca/TopStories/journalists-mar31.html* March 31, 1999.

IS IT NEWS OR ENTERTAINMENT?

While today's full-colour newscast looks like a million bucks — and often costs about that — there are nagging questions as to whether the old-style dedication is still there. Have news anchors become simply prime-time entertainers, and has the news become just a series of glib items cynically selected to entrance an audience that has a severely limited attention span?

One of the severest critics of today's TV newscasts is Frank Stalley, a former CBC *National* newsreader, now retired. Stalley, who was one of Canada's first network TV announcers, believes that today's reporters have become so immersed in the mystique of show business that facts now come far down on the list of priorities. "In addition," he says, "there's far too much editorializing in today's television news. We should go back to the time when the news announcer provided the straight story without such devices as the raised eyebrow or the inflection on a certain word to colour the viewer's impression."

Stanley Burke was one of CBC-TV's most colourful and controversial announcers — infamous for an on-air swearing session when technical problems piled up fast and furious one night. Burke agrees with Stalley to a point, and he's inclined to blame today's broadcast training schools for not quashing the seeds of the problem. But what's even more troublesome, says Burke, is that "there's not the dedication in today's newspeople. Many of them lack that fire in the belly that made some of us really work. We *cared* deeply about the medium and about our profession."

David Levy, CBC-TV's first correspondent in the Soviet Union, agrees that there's "too much emphasis on appearance and voice today. In the old days, it was what you had to *say* that mattered. People still remember my newscasts, because there was some substance." Burke concurs: "How long has it been since something on a newscast has made anyone say, 'Now *that's* a point I've never considered'?"

But Burke doesn't condemn today's anchors right across the board. "When I saw the movie 'Broadcast News,' I tended to feel a bit sorry for the pretty boy [played by William Hurt]. He was competent, and was *humble*. We in the news business are the most arrogant s.o.b.s who ever drew breath!" However, he says, the prevailing all-knowing attitude among news anchors inhibits many of them from exercising the vital ingredient of curiosity. These days, he says, "their attitude is 'Don't tell me . . . I'll tell *you*'."

Lloyd Robertson, the current dean of Canadian news anchors, took the middle-ground position on the subject of news as entertainment. "I think a news anchor should first of all be a good announcer," says Robertson. . . . "You have to deliver the material well or you've got nothing." Next in order of priority, he believes that "being a good reporter is important." He recalls a time when CBC-TV decided to make overnight on-camera stars out of "some very good newspeople." The camera terrified many of these neophytes into a state of suspended animation — and the experiment was dropped. "It was unfair to them, but it proved that you have to be both a reporter *and* an announcer to handle television," says Robertson, who stops short of using the word *entertainer*.

Source: John Porteous, "Is It News or Entertainment?" *TV Guide*, December 24, 1988, pp. 23, 24, and 27. Reprinted with permission from *TV Guide*, 1988 © TV Guide Magazine Group Inc.

NEGATIVE FACTORS: MORE HAPPY NEWS IS NOT THE ANSWER — WE WANT SOLUTIONS

There is considerable merit in what has become the standard public complaint about TV news and news generally, namely that it is preponderantly negative.

Even hardened news practitioners get sick of it, particularly when it involves personal vendettas against newsmakers whom the media itself [sic] promoted too heavily in the first place. The phenomena [sic] is most common when journalists begin to suspect that the political leaders they have been putting on pedestals, thoughtlessly, have feet of clay. Kim Campbell was the classic example.

But the replacement for such vindictive negativity should not be what the trade calls "happy news."

There's too much of that sort of banality around already: chit-chat at the anchor desk, soft features, and other forms of mindless infotainment.

And worthy as I find the movement at some local U.S. television stations to rid their "family sensitive" newscasts of violent visuals, I'm not sure that is the right basket in which to put all our eggs.

I'm all for getting rid of gratuitous violence on TV news. Do video clips of body bags, shrouded stretchers, and blood on the sidewalks really serve the viewing public? Or do they desensitize people to a point where gunshot wounds, for example, become an unremarkable urban experience?

It strikes me, however, that what is most often offensive about TV news is not what it puts on the air but what it doesn't. In a recent *Saturday Night* article on Eric Malling, host of CTV's *W5*, writer W.A. Szemberg summarized the TV journalist's opinion this way:

"Malling believes that people want to be told not how bad they are but how bad our problems are, and what can be done to solve them. Period."

Exactly.

Source: Peter Trueman, "Negative Factors: More Happy News Is Not the Answer — We Want Solutions," *Starweek Magazine*, January 2, 1995, p. 76.

PART 2

Radio

UNIT 6

The Radio News Script

18

Standard Layout

While there is no "standard layout" for radio news writing common to all stations, there are common elements in all scripts. Most newsrooms use computer programs to organize and format their scripts, so much of the layout is automatic. However, the computer can only do so much, and good writing and clear instructions are still the most important parts of radio copy.

Slugs and Mechanics

A slug line at the top or bottom of each story is a necessity. Most newsrooms require that the slug line contain a one- or two-word title for the story (called a slug, which gives the line its name), the date, the time of the newscast that the story is being written for, and the writer's name or initials. This information is either stacked in the upper left corner of the page

Hastings conviction
Sept. 12/96 . . . 5 p.m.
T. Placic

or written across the top or bottom of the page

Hastings conviction . . . Sept. 12/96 . . . 5 p.m. . . . TP.

Many newsrooms also require a notation to indicate which cart or carts (taped inserts) are contained in the story so that the newscaster or an operator can tell at a glance whether inserts are required and ensure that the right ones are loaded.

Hastings conviction . . . Cart 14
Sept. 12/96 . . . 5 p.m.
T. Placic

Hastings conviction . . . Sept. 12/96 . . . 5 p.m. . . . TP . . . Cart 14

As discussed in Chapter 4, most newsreaders prefer upper- and lower-case letters instead of all capitals. Always set the word processor not to hyphenate at the end of a line; hyphenated words are very difficult to read and often cause mispronunciations. Also, set the layout to triple space so that there is plenty of room to see each line clearly and lots of space to write in corrections or additions.

The "Reader"

A reader is a news story that does not have a taped insert; it is read entirely by the newscaster. While the majority of stories in a newscast are likely to be readers, it is important to remember that sound is radio's great advantage over newspapers. Having someone read a newspaper to you is not much of an improvement over reading it yourself — in fact, it's a lot less convenient and flexible. That's why taped inserts are so important for they add the sounds of the events and the voices of the participants to the basic description.

WHEN YOU TALK, DO PEOPLE LISTEN?

Radio news network is seeking applicants for anchor positions at its headquarters. We're looking for energetic, enterprising anchors with solid writing and production skills, a contemporary, conversational style, and the ability to touch an audience with relatable stories. Send résumés and tapes to. . . .

Exercise 18.1

As practice in writing readers, make these sets of facts into clear, well-written news stories. Remember to follow all the conventions and rules of broadcast copy (Chapters 4, 6, and 7) and to write a good lead (Chapter 5). If you are not using a computer that automatically adds a slug to the story, write your slug in the style favoured by your newsroom.

1. • Vincent Massey High School will be the setting for a movie.

   • The school will be taken over by the film crew for July and most of August. Scheduled summer school classes will be moved to Holy Name, across town.

   • The production is paying a substantial rent for the facilities, but both the school board and the producer, Greg Darling, have declined to say how much.

   • The film, called *Terror at Nightmare High*, is a production of Darling Films Ltd. from Toronto. It will star two unknown Canadian actors, Kelly Vasus and Jeffrey Norton, and be directed by a Canadian who lives in California, Jeff Woolnough.

   • Nearly all parts have been cast, but there may be some work for local people as extras.

2. • A 200-kilo black bear named Barney escaped from the city zoo last night.

   • An intensive "man"hunt went on throughout the night, involving the police department, The Humane Society, zoo officials, and volunteers. At one point, there were about 150 people involved in the search.

   • Suburban west side residents were told to stay indoors and to keep pets inside until the bear was recaptured, but at dawn he was still missing.

   • Finally, Barney was found at 8 a.m. curled up asleep in an unused building at the zoo. He was tranquilized and returned to his cage. Construction around the cage is still going on to make sure he can't get out again.

   • Barney is 9 years old and has been a resident of the zoo for 5 years.

3. • City council approved the education budget last night at its regular meeting.

   • Education subcommittee chair, Edna Prolattyn, recommended approval of the budget that features a 4% increase over last year.

   • The main cause of the increase is the school board's decision to offer early retirement to 100 teachers, and Councillor Prolattyn pointed out that this move would save the board more than $1,000,000 in the long run.

   • Other expenditures are being held to last year's levels, which means the requested expansion of Maple Grove school will be denied.

   • It is not known if this increase will mean a rise in municipal taxes, because other departmental budgets have not been presented yet.

The Teaser

A teaser is a headline-style sentence designed to attract an audience to tune in to a later newscast or to stay tuned during a commercial break in a newscast. Usually just one sentence long, a teaser is sometimes in the form of a sentence fragment, like newspaper headlines.

Some workers are still very unhappy after their strike is settled at a local auto plant.

New information surfaces in the city's longest murder investigation.

Great news for moms-to-be. . . . All coming up at six on the daily report.

In writing a teaser, you must try to sell the story by indicating why it might be of importance for the audience (remember the list of news values in Chapter 1) while not giving the entire story away. Avoid the oversensational style that is more typical of supermarket tabloids and American news magazine shows:

Blood in the streets! Swift justice! No sense of humour! All coming up at six on the daily report!

Teasers should contain some information that will make an audience want to stay tuned rather than suggestions of more drama or excitement than is actually in the story. Disappoint a listener once with a teaser and the sensationalism tactic won't work again. Good teasers are not easy to write; they take time and thought.

ARE YOU READY TO DO NEWS AS PART OF THE NEXT PREMIER MORNING SHOW IN THE COUNTRY?

If so, [radio station in _____] is looking for you! We're in search of the best news director on the planet. If you are organized, relate to women 18–34, and can deliver news that wakes up the greatest city in the country, we need to talk. This is your chance to work at a station on the grow in the country's best radio group. Get your tape and résumé yesterday to. . . .

Write teasers for each of the stories in Exercise 18.1 and for the three that follow.

1. A Quebec City resident visiting relatives here is in hospital after trying to prevent a moving car from running over a little girl. The man saw the parked car begin rolling down a slope toward the girl, who was playing in the street. He ran after the car and got the driver's door open, but in trying to get in he slipped under the wheels. He is in satisfactory condition with cuts and a broken ankle. The little girl is fine . . . the car missed her, then ran into a telephone pole.

2. One of this city's most popular teachers is not at work today . . . for the first time in 50 years. Harris Venturi has taught shop and math at Vincent Massey High School for the past half-century without ever missing a day . . . and yesterday he retired. More than 400 people attended a gala retirement party at the Ramada Hotel last night to wish him well. Many were former students, now with their own children and . . . in a couple of cases . . . grandchildren. Harris and his wife, Gina, were sent off on their retirement in style when they were given an all-expenses-paid cruise by their many friends and colleagues.

3. A local man is in custody after a holdup early this morning at the Convenience-Plus store on Elm Road. Police say that a man walked into the store and demanded money after showing the clerk a hunting knife. He took about 30 dollars from the cash register and ran away, but a passing police cruiser spotted him, and the officer pursued him. The arrested man is Wade Duggins of Cornwall Street. He is charged with robbery and weapons offences.

Assignments

1. In adding to your log (Review Assignments for Units One and Two), note which stories use taped inserts and which are readers. It is interesting to note the proportion of stories that contain inserts from station to station and from one time of day to another. Generally, you will notice that inserts are more common in stories broadcast in the morning. Why is this?

2. Many stations use teasers. It is a good idea to get into the habit of writing teasers for the top two or three stories of every newscast because you may be able to use them on the air but also because writing a teaser helps you to focus on what is really important and interesting about the story you are writing.

19

Writing to Sound

One of the primary skills of the radio newswriter is arranging taped inserts for the news story so that they are seamlessly interwoven with the voice of the newsreader. Regardless of the physical format of the insert (computer sound file, reel to reel, cassette, or cart), the same basic rules apply.

Hospital extension . . . April 19/95 . . . 6 p.m. . . . . GR . . . Cart 403

The city is finally going to get its hospital extension. The minister of health announced this morning that 32 million dollars is being allocated for the new wing. After five years of lobbying the government, Hospital Board Chair, Kathleen Verbeek, says she is satisfied . . .

Cart: 403
In: It's about time . . .
Out: . . . get started at last
Runs: 14 sec

Construction on the new geriatrics wing of City Hospital is expected to begin as early as next spring.

The notation "Cart:" is followed by an identifier for that specific cartridge or sound file. Some stations use a numbering system, while others label the cart or file with the story slug. "In:" is the incue: the first two or three words on the cart. Some stations omit this, but it does help the newscaster and operator to react instantly if the wrong insert is played. "Out:" is the outcue: the last two or three words on the cart. This is necessary so the newscaster knows when to resume reading. "Runs:" is the total running time of the insert in seconds. The newscaster needs this information so she or he knows how long is available for throat-clearing, sipping a drink, or previewing the next story.

If the outcue is repeated in the insert, it is necessary to note this so that the newsreader does not begin speaking when this cue is heard the first time but waits until the insert is actually over. For example, in the above story, Ms. Verbeek says at the end of the insert, "It'll be great to get started at last. I can't believe we're actually going to get started at last." The newsreader would probably begin speaking as soon as the outcue is heard, thereby interrupting Verbeek's last sentence. After the outcue, in such a situation, put in parentheses "double out" or "second time" (or whatever other notation is common at the station).

Cart: 403
In: It's about time . . .
Out: . . . get started at last (double out)
Runs: 14 sec

The Lead-In

The sentence in the news story immediately before the insert is called the "lead-in" (not to be confused with the "lead," the first sentence in the story). The lead-in must introduce the voice about to be heard on the insert. However, a good lead-in introduces the voice in such a way that *the story is complete even if the insert is not played*. When this is not done, the lead-in is called "blind," and it makes no sense unless the insert follows. Here are some examples:

Blind: Taxes may actually be going down. Mayor Collins explains. . . .
Better: Mayor Collins announced that taxes may actually be going down. . . .

Blind: Airport Manager Tyrone Percival tells us about his team's preparations . . . .
Better: Airport Manager Tyrone Percival says that snow removal is not a problem . . . .

Blind: After the loss, Coach Brant had this to say . . . .
Better: Despite the loss, Coach Brant is proud of his team . . . .

One of a newsreader's worst nightmares is that an insert does not play after it has been introduced. No matter how reliable the technology, sometimes something goes wrong, and it is the news anchor who sounds like a fool. Looking at these lead-ins, you can see how a blind lead-in would trap the newscaster, while the better ones would permit a graceful escape. A well-written lead-in should permit the reader to skip to the tag (the line after the insert) without the audience being aware that an insert should have played. Test your lead-ins by reading them followed immediately by the tag. The story should make sense.

ASSISTANT NEWS DIRECTOR/EDITOR-REPORTER

Immediate opening in a growing metropolitan newsroom. Position is responsible for day-to-day editing of reporters' materials, for assisting news director in running an active newsroom, and for researching, preparing, and reporting stories on a regular basis. Must have post-secondary journalism or related qualifications, clear, concise writing style, strong on-air presence, and knowledge of laws and regulations pertaining to journalism. Previous supervisory experience desirable. Salary depends on experience. Send tape, résumé, letter, and three references to. . . .

In addition to giving the newsreader an insurance policy against sounding foolish, lead-ins that aren't blind are much more stylish, giving the story a polished and professional sound.

The lead-in must also clearly identify the next voice to be heard. If the name of the person on the insert is mentioned a sentence or more before the voice is actually heard, then the audience will be confused about whose voice it is. Failing to identify the voice at all is, of course, worse. Identifying the voice after the cart is sometimes done, but it can be very confusing and can cause the audience to miss the importance of what was said. Another fault of some newswriters is to introduce the wrong voice or to give the names of two people in the lead-in. Which one are we listening to?

> **Wrong voice introduced:** Chief medical officer, Anne Powell, spoke with reporter Dan Skinner. . . .
> **Better:** Chief medical officer, Anne Powell, plans to take immediate action. . . .

In writing lead-ins, also avoid "parroting." This is repeating what is on the cart in the lead-in. If the cart with Anne Powell's voice began with the words "I plan to take immediate action," then the wording above would be parroting. The lead-in should add a fact to the story that will not be repeated word for word in the cart that follows. Naturally, one would expect Powell to say something about taking action — but not in the same words as the lead-in.

As a general rule, preview what is said on the insert and avoid repeating the person's first words.

Check each of these lead-ins to see if it measures up to the criteria discussed above. Improve those that are not perfect. Suggested answers begin on page 233.

1. Tony Jacobs is the site manager for the new building, and he says. . . .
   Cart: 21
   In: There is no problem . . .
   Out: . . . shouldn't collapse
   Runs: 10 sec

2. After a marathon discussion, council finally agreed to refer the budget back to committee. . . .
   Cart: 56
   In: I don't believe . . .
   Out: . . . terribly unfortunate
   Runs: 19 sec

3. Using the new computer system will save taxpayers millions of dollars, according to ministry spokesman Blair Robbins. . . .
   Cart: 250
   In: Using the new computer system . . .
   Out: . . . over the next ten years
   Runs: 25 sec

4. Geraldine Tremont is the owner of the flooded house, and she explains her point of view. . . .
   Cart: 04
   In: The damage is . . .
   Out: . . . city must help
   Runs: 35 sec

5. As she left the courthouse, Patricia McNaughton, lawyer for the accused, demanded a new trial. . . .
   Cart: 78
   In: There is now . . .
   Out: . . . to the Supreme Court
   Runs: 14 sec

The Tag

Finally, the line that the newsreader delivers after the cart is called a tag or a write-out. It rounds the story off, adding any information that has not been mentioned. It has another very useful function: it separates the story from the one to follow. Put yourself in the audience's position. A voice has just finished speaking, and now the newscaster is back on the air. Is she saying something about the current story, or has she begun a new one? If the lead of the new story is at all ambiguous, then it can seem to the audience that the story is just continuing after the cart. A tag allows the newscaster to bring the story to a close, to pause, to change pace or voice quality, and to begin the new story.

REPORTER/PRODUCER WANTED IN PROGRESSIVE, MIDMARKET, GROWING RADIO NEWSROOM

You're responsible for reporting, writing, producing, editing, and hosting live and recorded news and public affairs program materials. You have strong on-air presence, precise and clear writing skills, and a degree or diploma in journalism or broadcasting, and you understand journalism issues and ethics. You can thrive in a changing and diverse workplace and have an excellent grasp of today's news and of the background to current affairs. If you fit, we would like to hear from you. Send a tape, résumé, and letter to. . . .

Exercise 19.2

Write stories from the following facts, incorporating the taped inserts into the copy. Include a complete slug line, and remember what we have just discussed about lead-ins and tags.

1. • Denise Chabrier (SHA bree ay) is an exchange student from Lyon (LEE on), France, who is going home today after attending Pinetree College for the past two years in the Retail Management Program.
   • She is taking home many fond memories of her time in Canada, especially winter sports, friendly people, baseball, and Canada's multicultural personality.
   • While here, she stayed with a Canadian family, the Prestons on Lawrence Crescent, whose daughter, Janice, will be going to France to stay with Denise's family next summer and study French at a college in Lyon.
   • Denise's taped interview starts "I'll certainly miss . . ." and runs 17 seconds, ending " . . . back home." In the interview, she talks about meeting people from many different backgrounds while here and eating food from everywhere in the world, food which isn't as readily available in France.

2. • Workers at Steeltech Inc. have been on strike for two weeks, and there doesn't seem to be any end in sight as talks between the union and management have broken down.

• The issue is job security. The company wants to lay off 15% of its workforce (about 20 people) this year, while the union wants guarantees that no more than 5% will be let go each year for the next three years.

• There has been some trouble on the picket line, with truck drivers complaining they have been roughed up and picketers complaining they have been hit by incoming trucks that won't stop.

• Police are at the gates and monitoring the situation.

• A taped interview with Nick Bronski, a steelworker on the picket line, begins "We want to work . . ." and ends " . . . if we have to" and runs for 13 seconds. In it, Bronski says he's worried about his job, and so are all the other workers, some of whom have been at the company for 30 years. He's willing to take a pay cut but doesn't want to go on unemployment.

3. • Fred Justice has been the Member of Parliament for this area for the past 12 years, winning three elections for the N-D-P and serving as finance critic for the party in the House of Commons.

• He announced his retirement at a news conference this morning, citing health and family concerns as his reasons for leaving. He has been ill with severe arthritis for the past several years.

• A taped clip from his news conference begins "It has been . . . " and ends " . . . all the best" and runs for 28 seconds. In it, Justice says he has enjoyed serving the people of this city but now recognizes it is time to retire. It is at least two years before another election, so that will give the party time to find a candidate and begin preparations. He promises to work as hard as he is able to to get N-D-P members elected.

The Actuality

An actuality is the voice of a participant in the event. It may be the fire chief commenting on a stubborn fire, a politician talking about his party's leadership race, an angry striker on the picket line, or a witness of an accident or crime. The actuality can be obtained by a reporter on the scene using a small cassette recorder or by a telephone interview from the station. In either case, the "bite" or "clip," the short segment that is chosen for broadcast, will be transferred to cart or computer sound file. Then a story will be written that gives the details of the event, and, at an appropriate point in the story, the insert will be played, and the actuality will become part of the audience's overall impression of the news event.

Selecting the clip to use from an interview, conversation, or recording of a meeting or speech is sometimes a difficult task. As a rule, actualities should not be longer than 30 seconds. This limit varies from station to station. Some stations do not allow actualities to exceed 20 seconds. Others, such as the CBC, permit them to be virtually any length as long as valid information is being conveyed. People in the news do not all speak in convenient 30-second chunks. Some ramble on with complicated explanations, seldom coming directly to the point, while others, probably intimidated by the microphone, hardly say anything. Skilful reporters will ask and re-ask their questions in such a way as to limit the windbags and draw longer responses from the unwilling (see Chapter 8).

Reporters who have two hours of tape from which to select several actualities have another problem. How do you find the bit you want to use? The only answer is to play the tape over and over, noting on the tape counter where good possibilities occur. Journalists returning to the station from meetings or interviews often play cassettes over and over on their car stereos so that they become familiar with what was said and where the gold is among all the slag.

They are looking for a clear, concise statement that either summarizes the speaker's view or makes a dramatic or telling comment. It is important to remember that the actuality does not have to tell the story; the written copy that the newscaster will read does that. The actuality should add colour, drama, and interest as much as information. To hear a witness telling in her own words how she felt is a much more interesting actuality than having her describe what happened. The news copy can fill in the who, what, where, when, and how. The object is to take the audience to the event, to help them picture and feel what it was like to be there.

A reporter is expected to provide two or three or four useful actualities for each event covered. Subsequent newscasts sound terribly dull if the same actuality is heard time after time, so a reporter who covers any event is expected to produce several stories. This means finding several voice bits that meet the criteria of usable actualities.

Reporters can phone actualities in to the station using a variety of simple and easily obtainable connection devices that plug into a tape recorder. It is expected that the reporter will give the station staff clear instructions about the story's content as well as feed the actualities. At the station, the duty newswriter will record the actualities and write the copy along the lines suggested by the reporter. Normally, however, it is the reporter's responsibility to return to the station after an event to prepare the actualities and write the corresponding copy.

Reporter/Producer
Department: Programming
Reports to: News director
Supervises: None

Position summary:	Responsible for reporting, writing, producing, editing and hosting live and recorded news programs. Position is in a dynamic newsroom engaged in broad coverage of community issues.
Qualifications:	Postsecondary education in journalism, communications, or related field. Three years' experience in broadcast reporting and news operations. Knowledge of current affairs and journalism law. Ability to demonstrate highest-quality production skills.
Competencies and skills:	Thorough story planning and development. Careful research, editing, tape handling, copy writing, and board operating. Field reporting and sound gathering. Concise style. Strong on-air delivery.
Salary:	Dependent upon experience and education.
Date needed:	Immediately

Send cover letter, résumé and sample air-check tape to. . . .

The Voicer

A voicer is simply a report given by the reporter in his or her own voice. The reporter may be at the scene of a crime or accident, at the legislature or city hall, or even in the studio. Voicers are often ad libbed from sketchy notes rather than completely scripted. There should be some reason for the reporter to give the information in a voicer rather than simply write a story and let the newscaster tell it. Usually, the reason is that the reporter is on the scene and can describe what it is like to be there, giving immediacy to the report that would be absent if a newscaster read the story. (In some news organizations, especially in the United States, these "on the scene" voicers are called ROSRs, meaning "radio-on-scene reports.") Sometimes the reporter has been following the story and is an expert on what has happened, so it is natural that he or she tell the audience about it, even from a studio.

When a reporter does a voicer, she or he must still write a script for the newscaster to read, complete with lead, information, lead-in, and tag. As far as the newsreader is concerned, there is no difference between an actuality and a voicer except that the voice on the insert is that of a reporter instead of a participant. If a voicer is phoned in to the studio, then the on-duty newswriter will record the voice clip and write the copy for the newscaster. If the reporter has time to go back to the studio, having recorded a voicer on a tape recorder at the scene, then usually that reporter will prepare the insert and write the script.

Avoiding a blind lead-in to a voicer is tricky and requires some thought. Instead of saying "Here's reporter Vicki Thomas with the story," it is better to begin with "Reporter Vicki Thomas says the issue is not money but jobs." Many newswriters give up and use the blind lead-in with voicers because they are so difficult to avoid. *The key to a good lead-in for a voicer is to preview what the reporter will tell us.* Doing so makes a much more elegant and stylish sentence and provides an escape from the trap that a blind lead-in creates should the insert fail to run.

Blind: Reporter Virginia Chen is at the scene. . . .
Better: Reporter Virginia Chen says the fire is now under control. . . .

Blind: Reporter Barry Stanski has more. . . .
Better: According to reporter Barry Stanski, both west-bound lanes are blocked. . . .

Most often when a reporter does a voicer, she or he will end with a sign-off, also called direct close or standard close. It identifies the reporter, the station, and sometimes the location:

On the Drummond Freeway, this is Tanya Gordon for CK — .

or

Reporting for CK — News, this is Tanya Gordon.

or

Tanya Gordon, CK – News, on the Drummond Freeway.

The form of this close will normally be dictated by station policy, so each reporter will use the same signoff. In the outcue, this is indicated as "sign-off," "standard," or "direct" instead of the actual words spoken.

Major accident . . . Aug. 4/96 . . . 11 a.m. . . . DF . . . Cart 345

Traffic is at a standstill on the Drummond Freeway. Slippery conditions are being blamed for a chain reaction accident that involves as many as 100 vehicles. Reporter Tanya Gordon says the heavy rain is making things even worse. . . .

> Cart: 345
> In: There is no letup . . .
> Out: signoff
> Runs: 40 sec

The weather office says the storm should pass by midafternoon, and conditions will gradually improve.

Exercise 19.3

First, you are a reporter at the scenes of the following events. Write a voicer to send back to the station over the telephone for each of these stories. All the elements of good writing apply, including a good lead, correct format, and broadcast news style. End each voicer with your signoff.

Second, write the newsreader's copy for each of your voicers. Usually, this means saving a couple of facts from the story for the newsreader's introduction and tag. Work at avoiding the blind lead-in to your voicer.

A suggested version of the first story begins on page 233 to give you a model.

1. • Spring floods have washed out the bridge over nearby Rock River.
   • River Rd. is closed, and traffic is rerouted via Plane St.
   • Heavy rain combined with cold temperatures caused the flood, since ice jams, normally melted and cleared by now, have backed the water up.
   • The concrete bridge, more than 50 years old, collapsed when supports were washed away during the night.
   • City work crews will wait until at least tomorrow to assess the damage and decide if the bridge can be repaired.

2. • The city's United Way campaign officially ended at midnight last night.
   • The goal of $1.8 million was met — the 4th time in a row the goal has been achieved, but it came down to the wire this time.

• A last-minute donation of $7,000 by the Lions Club put the fund over the top.

• The gift was greeted with cheers since campaign officials had gathered at campaign headquarters, ready to announce a shortfall.

• United Way donations are used to assist more than 40 local charities.

3. • Holy Name High School's production of *Anne* debuted last night to a sold-out audience in the school auditorium.

• The play is a musical based on *Anne of Green Gables* but is brought forward into the 1990s.

• It was written in a collaboration by the grade 12 drama class under the direction of dramatic arts teacher Valerie McHayle.

• It stars grade 12 student Joyce Reece in the title role and has a cast of almost 50 students from all grades, with an orchestra of 40.

• The play has been an all-year project, with planning starting in September and rehearsals under way by Feb.

• It runs tonight and tomorrow. Showtime is 7:30, and a few tickets are left.

The Wrapper

Wrap-around or V/A reports are a combination of the voicer and the actuality (hence the term V/A). In a wrapper, the audience hears the newscaster first, then the reporter, then a participant, then the reporter again for a signoff, and finally the newscaster again for a tag. Transcribed, it sounds like this:

Newscaster [live]
It didn't take the newest member of city council long to make her presence felt. Reporter Jian Lee says that the rookie councillor is concerned about proposed zoning changes in her neighbourhood. . . . [cart begins]

Reporter [on cart]
When Barbara White was elected to council in a special by-election two weeks ago, everyone expected her to stand up against more development in Ward Three . . . that's the platform that got her elected. But no one expected a confrontation quite so early. White moved a resolution at last night's meeting to stop all zoning changes in the city until a complete review of the city's master plan has been completed. The quiet council meeting erupted as several of the pro-development councillors took their shots. Councillor White seemed unperturbed by it all. . . .

White [on same cart]
Well, I felt it was something that had to be done sometime, so why not get it out of the way early? They can't just go putting up high-rise buildings wherever they want when the people who live in these neighbourhoods want low-density housing. We have a master plan, so let's find out if it's still useful, and if it's not let's scrap it and put a new one in place.

Reporter [on same cart]
The result of the uproar was a vote of 12 to five in favour of White's motion. All development is put on hold until at least next fall, when the report on the master plan is expected. At City Hall, I'm Jian Lee for CK — news. [cart ends]

Newscaster [live]
So far there has been no reaction from Giant Holdings Incorporated, the developer of the proposed high-rise complex.

The copy that the newsreader would get for this story is only this:

Development vote . . . Nov. 23/99 . . . 6 p.m. . . . Lee . . . Cart 48

It didn't take the newest member of city council long to make her presence felt. Reporter Jian Lee says that the rookie councillor is concerned about proposed zoning changes in her neighbourhood . . .

> Cart: 48
> In: When Barbara White . . .
> Out: signoff
> Runs: 55 sec

So far there has been no reaction from Giant Holdings Incorporated, the developer of the proposed high-rise complex.

Wrappers are not as common as voicers or actualities for the simple reason that they are harder to do and take more time. However, experienced reporters use them to produce a full, interesting, professional news story.

Exercise 19.4

Write the copy that the newsreader might get for each of the following wrappers. A suggested version for the first story begins on page 234 to give you a model.

1. • Reporter Kevin Horvath has a story about the new computers that are being installed in city police cruisers. He talks about what they will do, from checking ownership of vehicles, to displaying information about

people who have warrants out for their arrest, to telling the officer if someone hasn't paid parking fines.

• The actuality is Sergeant Vivian Lebrun, who has just returned from a training course in Montreal, where she learned all about the computers, and who is going to be training the force's officers in their use. She is very excited about the way they will improve the efficiency of police personnel on patrol assignments.

• Horvath's incue is "When an officer . . . ," and he signs off at the end of the report, which is 55 seconds long.

2. • Reporter Maria Cellini was at the fire that destroyed a family home at 56 Whiteside Avenue. She talks about the smouldering ruins and the fact that nothing is left of the two-storey frame house. The owners, Jack and Yolande Gervais, were not at home at the time. She adds that no cause has been finally determined, but suspicions focus on a wood stove in the living room.

• The actuality is of Fire Chief Harold Timlin, who says that the fire was so well established by the time the alarm came in that all his people could do was prevent it from spreading to nearby houses.

• Cellini's incue is "There is nothing . . . ," and she signs off at the end of the report, which is 47 seconds long.

3. • Reporter Reeta Washington describes the drowning of two local youngsters who were swept into a drainage culvert during spring flooding. The two boys, aged 9 and 11, were playing by a ditch when one fell in and the other tried to rescue him. The bodies have now been recovered, but the names of the boys have not been released. She points out that warnings have been issued to parents to keep their kids away from any drainage areas at this time of year because of the dangers of fast-moving water.

• The actuality is Tammi Richards, a 10-year-old from the neighbourhood who knew the boys and often played with them. She says that kids often play down by the ditch but that nothing bad has happened before.

• Washington's incue is "There is a sense . . . ," and she signs off at the end of the report, which is 41 seconds long.

Exercise 19.5

You are a reporter. Write the script you would record to produce a wrapper for the following stories. When you finish your own script for each, write the newscaster's script to introduce and tag your report. A suggestion for the first story begins on page 234 as a model.

1. • The Hawks have just been eliminated from the semifinals of the provincial basketball championships. The Vincent Massey High School team was favoured to win and go on to the finals, but they lost 86–80 to St. Joseph's school from _____ (another city in the province).

   • This is the second year the Hawks got this far, and both times they were eliminated by St. Joseph's. The high scorer for the Hawks was Hank Roiton with 19 points.

   • Coach Danny Steinbach is very disappointed. His actuality begins "We had it . . ." and ends ". . . maybe next year"; it runs nine seconds.

2. • A local man has been found not guilty of armed robbery in a trial that concluded today.

   • George McInnis of Main St. had been arrested for the July 7th holdup of a downtown furniture dealer. The masked thief held the manager at gunpoint and took about $400 from the cash drawer.

   • The defence claimed that it was a case of mistaken identity and produced a witness who said she was with McInnis at the time of the robbery. McInnis was arrested after a week-long investigation by city police. They now say they have no other suspects.

   • The actuality is of George McInnis saying that he is happy to be free to get on with his life after this terrible ordeal. It starts "After all . . ." and ends ". . . ever again" and runs for eleven seconds.

3. • The band Yellow Fever will be playing at the Pinetree College arena tonight to a sell-out crowd. The 8000 seats were sold within hours of becoming available last week, and organizers tried to get a second concert, but the band had other commitments.

   • Their recently released album, *Malaria*, has gone gold in Canada and is doing well in the United States. The 12-person band is on a concert tour of 12 U.S. cities, including Chicago, L.A., Baltimore, and Houston, and is making stops in 5 Canadian cities.

   • In his actuality, lead guitarist Tyrone Lestat calls their music a fusion of rock, new age, jazz, and classical. He says the reason for their rising popularity is simply that this is good music well played. The tape is 26 seconds. and begins "Our sound . . ." and ends ". . . hard to explain."

Live Reports

Cellular and satellite phones permit on-scene reporting virtually anywhere. If a reporter can get to the event, then she or he can call back and go on-air live. Naturally, there must be careful co-ordination of timing; the reporter will call in just before a scheduled newscast and wait until the newscaster provides an introduction. Live reports, like voicers, are often ad libbed from rough notes rather than read from a complete script. Often they take the form of a question-and-answer conversation with the newscaster. If time permits, the reporter will tell the newsroom which questions the newscaster ought to ask, thus ensuring that the reporter is not asked a question for which she or he has no answer — a potentially embarrassing situation.

Some reporters are very uncomfortable with live reports and insist on calling in a few minutes before the newscast with a voicer instead of risking a live performance. Some newscasters are similarly uncomfortable about such live events. While a voicer does sound more polished, the spontaneity of a live report can emphasize radio's other great advantage over print: immediacy.

Unit Six
Review Exercises

Here are some more stories that you can use to practise your skills in writing to sound. Don't forget to use slug lines for all stories.

1. Write the newsreader's copy.

   - Reporter Drew vanDamm has sent a voicer (30 seconds) about a strike at a local printing plant, Inkspot Inc.
   - In the voicer, he describes the dispute and the history of negotiations, ending in the strike that began this morning. Incue: It has been . . . . Signoff.
   - Additional information: the plant publishes 3 local papers: the *Northern Weekly*, the *Advertising Review*, and the *City Express*. All have made arrangements to publish elsewhere, but subscribers may experience delays.

2. Write the newsreader's copy.

   - At last night's local school board meeting, discussion centred on the provincial guidelines for sex education in secondary schools.
   - Several parents spoke against the teaching of sex education, complaining that it provides sex instruction and encourages premarital sex among high school students.
   - Two teachers spoke in support of the guidelines.
   - No vote was held, but school board officials agreed to arrange a special information forum on the guidelines with provincial officials present so that concerns can be expressed.
       Tape: Mrs. Evelyn Creemore (14 seconds) doesn't want sex taught in schools — parents must decide when children are ready for such information.
       Incue: We are outraged . . .
       Outcue: . . . from now on
       Tape: Lorna Matyzk (MATCH ik) (19 seconds) teaches sex education and wants young people to have information to make choices instead of doing something stupid through ignorance.
       Incue: Since when . . .
       Outcue: . . . age of AIDS

3. a. Write the *reporter's* copy for a voicer.
   b. Write the *newsreader's* copy for the same voicer.

   - The scene is the grand opening of the new Downtown Shopping Centre.
   - Mayor David Pirelli has just cut the ribbon to officially open the 60-store mall, right in the downtown core opposite City Hall.
   - It took two years to build the centre, and it's now fully operational and already crowded with shoppers.
   - Also on hand for the opening are Flora White, MLA for the local riding, and Herman Gretzinger, president of Mallmen Enterprises, the builders and owners.
   - The centre includes office space, ample underground parking, 2 restaurants, a fitness club, and 4 movie theatres.

4. a. Write the *reporter's* copy for a wrapper.
   b. Write the *newsreader's* copy for the same wrapper.
   Use the information contained in Review Exercise 3 and include the following actuality.

   Tape: Mayor David Pirelli (22 seconds) talks about revitalizing the downtown area and making the city a vibrant, exciting, and safe place to live and shop.
   Incue: It gives me great . . .
   Outcue: . . . our wonderful city

5. a. Write the *reporter's* copy for a wrapper on the stories in Review Exercise 2.
   b. Write the *newsreader's* copy for the same wrappers.

PART 3

Television

UNIT 7

The Television Script

20

Writing to Visuals

The Split Page

Television is a team medium. Even in the simplest newscast, there will be a reader (or anchor), a director (who may also do the switching), a script assistant, an audio person, a teleprompter operator, and a videotape operator, all of whom need scripts. These scripts must have the words the anchor will read. They must also have clear notations of the other elements — audio, pictorial, or both — that will be used in the newscast and how they are to be inserted. Everyone on the team must know what is expected and what is going on at all times. Many different script formats have been tried over the years, and several different ones are still used; however, most have a common feature: *they are split down the middle, with the newsreader's copy on the right and all audio and video instructions on the left of the page.*

At the top of the page, there is space for a notation of the story's one- or two-word title (called a slug), the writer's name, the date, and the time of the newscast. Any one of the many computer programs used in newsrooms will prompt the writer for this information and then display it at the top of the page. If a video insert is used, many scripts will have the video file's or cassette's identification at the top of the page as well. This information allows the videotape operator (and others) to tell at a glance which stories have inserts with them and which footage goes with which story.

Snowmobile death
Jan. 22 . . . 11 p.m. . . . Giganti

NEWSCASTER O/C

NEWSCASTER O/C
A Highland man is dead as the result of a snowmobiling accident. Gerard Proton of Station Street was killed when his snow-mobile crashed through the ice on Trout Creek this afternoon. Proton was found within an hour of the accident by a group of skiers who happened to be following his trail. The Ministry of Natural Resources has issued several warnings about thin ice this week, following a spring thaw that has left many waterways very dangerous.

The notation "NEWSCASTER O/C" tells everyone on the crew that during this story the anchor will be reading O/C, on camera. It appears on both sides of the page to prevent any confusion. The right side is fed into the teleprompter, where it is projected onto the lens of the camera and read by the anchor. *Any notations that affect the anchor, therefore, should appear there along with the script.* As far as the script on the right-hand side of the page is concerned, the rules of good broadcast writing do not change, regardless of the margins or the medium.

Terminology

In order to write the instructions for the crew down the left side of the page, a TV writer must know the tools that are available and the terminology that is understood by everyone on the crew. Unfortunately, there are no universals: every station uses a slightly different set of terms depending on the equipment it has available and the preference of the news director. Fortunately, it does not take long to adapt to the terms in use at the station where you are writing. The following is a list of terms that includes most of the short forms and notations in common use.

O/C	Means "on camera" and indicates that the image of the reader appears in the frame. The name of the person who is O/C will be placed beside the notation so there is no confusion when two anchors are used.
V/O	Means "voice over"; the anchor continues to read the script over still or video images from the story. Again, the name of the reader who is doing the V/O should be written beside the notation.
SOT	Means "sound on tape" and is a videotape insert including the audio. Incues and outcues are given along with the running time of the insert.
VTR	Stands for "videotape recording" and is a videotape insert without sound. Often the additional notation of **SIL** is added so there is no confusion (i.e., **SILVTR**).
STILL	Refers to a still picture. Some stations called it **SLIDE**, while others use the name of the equipment used to project it (e.g., **ADDA**).
CG	Means "character generator," which is a device for printing letters across the screen. It is usually used to provide the names of people on camera. In some stations, it is called **FONT** or **TITLE**.
KEY	Means "chromakey" and refers to the technique of projecting an image electronically on a blue or green screen behind the newscaster.
BOX	Is a graphic box that can be placed anywhere on the screen and filled with a graphic or an image. It is normally used in conjunction with the term KEY. For example, "KEY BOX of STILL" means that a still picture would appear in a box somewhere on the screen beside the newscaster.
B/G	Is the notation for "background" and is usually used as an audio instruction. For example, "SOT . . . AUDIO B/G for Announcer's V/O" means that the audio on a videotape is played in the background while the announcer does a voice over.

These terms and the ability that you have already developed in writing for the ear and using broadcast newswriting conventions, plus same practice, are all you need to write for TV news. Study these examples and visualize what will appear on the screen in each case.

Local Champ
Mar. 1 . . . 11 p.m. . . . G.R.
VTR: 55 sec

VALERIE O/C	VALERIE O/C
	One member of the highly rated Canadian speed-skating team at this year's World Championships is a local man. Dennis Blanchard is a one-thousand-metre specialist whose performance this year indicates he may be in line for a medal. Third in his last two races in Europe, Blanchard is skating like never before. . . .
SOT: 55 sec	
SUPER: "Dennis Blanchard"	
IN: I'M VERY HAPPY . . .	IN: I'M VERY HAPPY . . .
OUT: . . . THIS YEAR	OUT: . . . THIS YEAR
RUNS: 55 sec	RUNS: 55 sec
VALERIE O/C	VALERIE O/C
	Blanchard will skate in both the one-thousand-metre sprint and the men's relay on Wednesday.

In the above script, the anchor (Valerie) will read the copy while her head and shoulders appear on camera. When she reaches the words "never before," a tape of Dennis Blanchard speaking will replace her on the screen and will run for 55 seconds. At the director's command, the words "Dennis Blanchard" will be superimposed at the bottom of the screen to identify the speaker, and they will disappear when the director decides to remove them. At the end of the tape (the last words are "this year"), the anchor will reappear on camera for a three-line tag.

Train Wreck
July 23 . . . 12 noon . . . Cassidy
SILVTR: 30 sec
SOT: 12 sec

TINA O/C	TINA O/C Emergency crews are at the scene of a train derailment on the west side of the city. A 60-car freight train carrying cars and machinery went off the rails at 9 this morning.
SILVTR: 30 sec TINA V/O CG: "This morning"	TINA V/O Fortunately, all the cars remained upright, and damage was limited. However, the main C-N-R rail line between here and Win nipeg has been shut down until the wreck age can be cleared and the track repaired. Transport Canada officials are on the scene trying to determine the cause of the mishap. A witness of the accident . . . Uta Glasser . . . was looking out the front win dow of her Station Street home when the slow-moving train left the tracks . . . .
SOT: 12 sec IN: THE NOISE WAS OUT: SMOKE AND DUST RUNS: 12 sec TINA O/C	IN: THE NOISE WAS OUT: SMOKE AND DUST RUNS: 12 sec TINA O/C Two of the train's crew were shaken up, but their injuries are minor.

Here the anchor (Tina) reads four lines while on camera and then continues to read while a silent videotape runs for 30 seconds. The words "This morning" are superimposed at the bottom of the screen. The anchor's voice and the silent tape end at the same time, and a tape with Uta Glasser's observations appears on screen for 12 seconds. When it ends, the anchor reappears to deliver a two-line tag. Clearly, timing is very important here. The writer has provided exactly enough words for Tina to read in order to fill the 30 seconds that the silent tape will run. This writer has estimated Tina's reading speed at about two and a half seconds per line. This speed will vary with the reader and with the margin widths accepted by different teleprompters.

New Park
Aug. 12 . . . 10 p.m. . . . G.D.V.
SOT: 1:20

KEVIN O/C KEY BOX: STILL "Coat of Arms"	KEVIN O/C Highland Avenue residents are finally going to get their park and playground. City council voted 12 to six last night in favour of a motion to create Highland Park on the corner of Tenth Avenue.
SOT: 1:20 AUDIO B/G FOR KEVIN V/O	KEVIN V/O The homeowners' association has been lobbying council for more than four years trying to get the vacant parcel of land . . . which is owned by the city . . . turned into a playground. Spokesperson for the group . . . Vern Taylor . . . says the lot is
AT 20 sec AUDIO UP CG: "Highland St. Resident Vern Taylor"	now just a garbage dump and hangout. . . .
IN: WE ARE VERY CONCERNED	IN: WE ARE VERY CONCERNED
OUT: THIS DECISION RUNS: 60 sec KEVIN O/C	OUT: THIS DECISION RUNS: 60 sec KEVIN O/C Construction on the new park is expected to begin next week.

In this script, the anchor appears on camera with a graphic box beside and behind his head with a picture of the city coat of arms in it. Five lines into the script, a videotape with sound begins, but the audio person is instructed to keep the sound volume down so the anchor can continue to read his V/O. At 20 seconds (eight lines of script), the audio volume is brought up, and the audience hears the words of Vern Taylor. At the bottom of the screen, the words "Highland St. Resident Vern Taylor" appear. The tape lasts for 80 seconds in total, so the voice portion runs for exactly a minute. When it ends (with the words "this decision"), the anchor reappears to deliver a two-line tag. Again, timing is critical because, if the anchor reads more slowly than estimated, when the sound on the tape is brought up it will cut into what Vern Taylor is saying. On the other hand, if the anchor is faster than estimated, the sound will come up before Taylor begins to speak.

The Lead-In

The sentence just before an SOT insert is called a lead-in. In radio, the lead-in should not be "blind" — that is, it should not be phrased in such a way that the tape must follow, just in case there is a technical fault and it jams or isn't cued. If this happens, the radio anchor can go on with the story, with his or her credibility intact and the audience none the wiser. In TV, if a tape insert doesn't run, everyone knows. The audience watches the anchor get more and more uncomfortable as the delay goes on and then, when hope is gone, apologize and go on with the next story. Therefore, the practical reason for avoiding blind lead-ins doesn't exist in television. However, the complete-sentence lead-in that adds an item of information to the story instead of merely announcing that a bite is coming is elegant and stylish. It should be used whenever possible. Refer to Chapter 19 for more information and exercises on avoiding the blind lead-in.

Also avoid writing too closely to the insert. This is writing a lead-in that begins a sentence that will be completed on the video file or tape or asking a question that will be answered on the insert.

> It's been a long day for the firefighters. Chief Grantham says they are . . . [roll tape].

> Reporter Janice Veletti was at the meeting. When will we get a decision, Janice? [roll tape]

In each case, the writing is too close to the insert. Even a short delay between the anchor's lead-in and the beginning of the video file or tape will cause an awkward and distracting break, making everyone on the crew look bad. Alternatives to these lead-ins that add a fact to the story are much superior.

It's been a long day for the firefighters. Chief Grantham says his crew is exhausted. [roll tape]

Reporter Janice Veletti was at the meeting. She tells us that a decision will be announced soon. [roll tape]

In writing the lead-in, also be careful not to parrot the words on the SOT. It sounds silly to have the anchor say "In Ottawa, the finance minister said the report was just speculation" and then have the insert begin with the finance minister saying "That report is just speculation."

The Tag Line

After an SOT insert, the newscaster may come back O/C to deliver a line that concludes or rounds off the story. This is called a tag. Tags are not as important in TV as they are in radio because in television the end of a story is more clearly conveyed. Nonetheless, many news directors like to end a bite with a tag. It finishes the story off and can make a smooth segue to the next story.

Exercise 20.1

The following are the audio portions (right-hand column) of television news stories. Each is followed by a list of the visual elements available for the story. Write the complete script, right-hand and left-hand columns, inserting the visuals to make an interesting presentation of the story. Change the scripts if you want in order to accommodate your visuals better.

1. A local farmer is experimenting with an unusual . . . but potentially very valuable . . . new crop. Mesha Bakravan grew tobacco on his 50-hectare farm until two years ago, when he decided to try something different as the market for tobacco declined. Now he is growing ginseng. Ginseng is a medicinal plant that is used around the world, but chiefly in Asia, where it has been a valuable crop since ancient times. Made into a tea or syrup, it is supposed to cure all sorts of ailments and is even reputed to help keep you young. There are now dozens of ginseng growers in Canada, most of them in Ontario, and the ginseng they produce is . . . according to the Chinese importers . . . the best in the world.

    Visuals: SOT of Bakravan explaining the difficulties of growing ginseng. SILVTR of the farm and workers caring for the plants. Any graphics you want.

2. A computer malfunction in Ottawa is being blamed for the delay in distributing unemployment insurance cheques this week. The local employment office was swamped with calls yesterday and again today as anxious people phoned in to find out what had happened to their allowances. Yvonne Deschamps, the manager of the office, says that the problem is expected to be corrected by tomorrow. Meanwhile, the delay means real hardships for some of the city's unemployed. Ruth-Anne Hasselby was laid off from her job six weeks ago and counts on the weekly cheque to pay for necessities. Officials estimate that there are about ten thousand people in the city who rely on unemployment insurance cheques for some or all of their daily needs.

   Visuals: SOT of Deschamps describing the problem and asking people to be patient. SOT of Hasselby describing how she is managing without the cheque. SILVTR of lineups at the employment office. STILL of an unemployment insurance cheque with the word *Delayed* written across it. Any CG you want.

3. Pinetree College has closed its popular Theatre Arts Program as a cost-cutting measure. The surprise announcement was made this morning by the college president, Martha Whitman. However, students have already mobilized to protest the decision and to try to save the program. The leader of the students is Barry Pleasance, a second-year student in scenic design. He says that, while it's true the program is expensive to run, it provides much-needed training for theatre technicians across Canada and serves the local community. This afternoon's rally attracted about 200 students and was addressed by Alderman James Massey, who encouraged them to keep the pressure on. A mass protest is scheduled for tomorrow in front of the administration building.

   Visuals: SOT of Whitman saying that she regretfully had no choice but to cut the program because of the expense of maintaining a separate campus for the theatre. SOT of Pleasance saying that not enough had been done to raise funds to keep the program open and calling on all levels of government to help. SOT of the students protesting today and Massey saying that the program is vital to the cultural well-being of the community. STILL of the college crest. Any CG you want.

Exercise 20.2

Use the elements in the following story outlines to write polished, visually interesting television news stories.

1. • The mayor cut the ribbon this morning to open a new factory in town.

   • Vectortrim Ltd. will make luxury exercise and fitness equipment for the home and club markets. The company already has a small plant in

Sherbrooke, Quebec, and the new plant will supply the western and export markets.

• The factory is in a building on Church Street that was formerly a shoe and boot factory but has been empty for the past 8 years. For the first year, about 20 people will be employed, but if the American market opens up as anticipated, capacity will be increased, and about 30 additional jobs will result.

• Vectortrim is owned by Dan and Vera Yatellin and has been making gym equipment for 12 years.

• You have unlimited silent videotape of the factory and the opening ceremony, including the mayor and the owners shaking hands and cutting the ribbon.

• You have SOT of an interview with Dan Yatellin talking about the factory and his plans for the future.

• You have SOT of the mayor (Gerta Plavcek) while she works out on one of the Vectortrim rowing machines. She welcomes the business to town, wishes it well, and hopes that it may have an influence on her own fitness program.

2. • Terence Harper, 51, of Garner Ave., was killed this morning when the forklift truck he was operating at Stanley Metals Ltd. rolled over after being struck by a piece of heavy machinery.

• According to police, the forklift was in a restricted area of the factory on West 10th St. and was driven into the path of a 200-tonne crane.

• Harper had worked at Stanley Metals for the past 27 years. He was married and had three children, all living away from home.

• Harper was pulled from the wreckage of his forklift by firefighters using the Jaws of Life apparatus and was rushed to City General Hospital, where he was pronounced dead from head injuries.

• You have SOT of an interview with the factory manager, Neil O'Reilly. He says no one understands why Harper drove into the dangerous area near the crane. He was an experienced worker and knew the danger. O'Reilly concludes by saying that everyone is very upset and saddened by the death of a popular co-worker.

• You have a photograph of Harper taken two years ago for a newspaper story about his 25th anniversary at Stanley Metals.

• You have file footage (videotape that has been stored in the station's library) of the interior of Stanley Metals but no sound.

3. • The local Rotary Club is welcoming a student from France on an exchange program. The Rotary Club sponsors international student exchanges, arranging for accommodation and living expenses while the student is in the country studying.

• Jean-Marc Jarre, 17, is from Dijon, France, and is in grade 12. He hopes to be an architect. He will be in Canada for 12 months, attending Vincent Massey High School.

• Helen Lanchyshyn of Main St. spent last year in Dijon, where she attended high school as part of the same program. She returned in August and is now attending Pinetree College.

• You have SOT of an interview with Jean-Marc in which he thanks the Rotary Club for making the exchange possible and says that he is looking forward to studying with Canadian students and learning about their country. He concludes by saying that he is especially looking forward to a Canadian winter.

• You have SOT of the president of the local Rotary Club, Morris Oxford, who welcomes Jean-Marc and says that Rotary International is delighted to promote international understanding by having young people visit each other's country.

• You have a still photograph of Helen Lanchyshyn.

Exercise 20.3

Record an entire television newscast. From the newscast, pick out three stories that range from visually very simple and straightforward to very complex. For each of the three stories, transcribe the anchor's script and, using it as your right-hand column, write in the visual cues that would produce the story.

Assignments

1. At least once a week, record an entire local TV newscast. Play it back, taking note of the visual elements used in the stories, the number of cameras used in the newsroom itself, the style of lead-in to SOT favoured in this newsroom, and the number of SILVTR segments used with V/O. If any mistakes occur, can you figure out what went wrong? Such careful analysis of TV news packages will enable you to understand much better how the newsroom works and how to write effectively for TV news.

2. Request permission to spend a day observing the preparation of the daily newscast at a local station. Prepare a report that outlines the chronology of the day, lists the personnel involved and their functions, notes the problems encountered and how they were overcome, and fully explains your own observations. Include a videotape of the resulting newscast.

21

Television Reporting

The following two chapters deal with all aspects of reporting for television news. In this chapter, we will look at the principles and fundamentals of TV reporting, and in Chapter 22 we will examine in more detail the skills and techniques needed to be a videographer. Since the functions of reporter and videographer overlap and complement one another, these two chapters should be considered together. Indeed, the two professions often blend and merge in practice.

ENG Basics

Electronic news gathering (ENG) is the term that is applied to television news reporting. At large stations and networks, an ENG crew might consist of a reporter, a producer, a camera person, and a sound person, and maybe even a lighting technician. At smaller stations, it is becoming common for an ENG crew to consist of one person who performs all these functions: the videographer. While equipment varies widely, there are some principles of good ENG production that we can discuss, regardless of the hardware being used. With a full crew, most production decisions are not the reporter's responsibility; however, it is extremely important that a reporter earn the respect and co-operation of the crew. Establish a reputation as a hard-working, co-operative, appreciative, quality-conscious professional and any crew will do its best for you. Solicit and take the advice of the crew. A reporter who has the attitude that he is in charge and makes all the decisions risks alienating the very people who can make him look good and loses the chance to benefit from the experience and insight of the crew.

The Stand-Up

The stand-up is the aptly named field production of a reporter speaking directly into the camera, usually while standing in front of something that pertains to the story. It is often used as part of a package that includes bites of interviews or footage of the event itself; however, the entire report of an event can be done in the form of a stand-up, particularly if a late-breaking story doesn't allow time for a polished and edited package. The stand-up may introduce the package and conclude it, or it may act as a bridge between two bites.

When the stand-up is to be part of a package, it presents an interesting challenge, because the stand-up is recorded in the field along with the other footage that will be edited into the finished story and must fit into the package. In other words, *the stand-up must be delivered in such a way that it fits in with a story that hasn't been written yet.* The reporter must have a clear idea of the shape of the entire story and a pretty solid concept of how the stand-up will fit in with the other elements of the story.

Stand-ups are typically between 15 and 30 seconds long and must be memorized or ad libbed from notes. This is a special skill and may take time to develop. Even the most seasoned reporters will typically do three or four retakes to get a stand-up just right.

It is critical that the stand-up be more than just a talking head; there should be some justification for having the reporter on camera. Usually, stand-ups are used because they are the quickest and easiest way to tell the story without just giving the anchor a reader. Moreover, many news directors like to establish their reporters and give them exposure in their communities, so stand-ups are favoured. But just putting a reporter on camera is not very interesting unless he or she is clearly on location and actively involved in the story. A background of a political convention, a war zone, a traffic wreck, or a hockey practice adds credibility to what the reporter says about that event. A stand-up recorded in front of a neutral background such as a brick wall, a generic parking lot, or (worse) a studio is pointless.

Tip 1. *Dress neatly and make sure you are well groomed.* Messy hair, dirty sneakers, or inappropriate clothing will destroy credibility and distract your audience.

Tip 2. *There is no need to announce where you are.* Let the shot or the anchor's introduction handle that. To say "I'm here inside the cattle ring at the Lincoln County Fair" is to state the obvious and insult the viewers' intelligence.

Posting Date:
Position: Writer/reporter
Location:
Salary: Commensurate with qualifications and experience
Hours of work: 40 hours per week on rotating shifts. Overtime as required based on operational needs.

Responsibilities:
- contributes to news programs by writing news stories, voice overs, and intros to reports
- monitors news feeds for appropriate video and news stories to be used in newscasts derived from newswires and local sources
- searches computer files and videotapes for footage
- lines up the news stories for the newscasts and splits, ensures all information is listed on scripts for anchors, master, and production, and distributes copies
- works with editors to determine what can be edited out or modified in a story when necessary
- will act as a backup producer for all newscasts
- must be able to gather, write, and voice news reports
- other duties as required

Qualifications:
- extensive experience in broadcast writing
- postsecondary education in journalism, broadcast newswriting
- in-depth knowledge of local region, national and international news, and current affairs
- experience in producing and reporting
- proven ability to prioritize and meet deadlines of several simultaneous duties while maintaining focus and composure
- proven ability to marry picture and sound
- excellent communication skills — both oral and written
- ability to work in a team and be self-motivated
- practical working knowledge of computer office systems
- good understanding of journalistic ethics

Application Details: Interested candidates are encouraged to forward a current résumé and audition tape in confidence.

Deadline:

Tip 3. *Practise with the microphone.* Learn where to hold it for the best sound quality and how to hold it so that it doesn't interfere with gestures, props, or clipboard.

Tip 4. *Never take your eyes from the camera lens during a stand-up except for a deliberate and rehearsed movement.* Reporters who cannot hold their eyes steady on the camera look nervous, shifty, and amateurish.

The Package

This is television's "wrapper" (see Chapter 19) and includes any number of elements, usually edited together into a package that is introduced and tagged by the anchor. A typical package might open with a reporter's voice-over tape of the event followed by an SOT interview with a participant in the event, and a short stand-up to close. Many are far more complex than this simple model, involving natural (or wild) sounds, several SOT segments, silent footage, and a couple of short stand-ups to bridge the pieces. Such packages are so common in TV news now that they are virtually the standard method of covering events at many larger stations and networks. The anchor, in many instances, is not much more than a bridge between packages. However, packages do require time — to shoot, to plan and write, to edit. Stations that expect two or three or more stories from each crew cannot permit many packaged reports.

Most TV operations require reporters to hand over a complete shot list with editing instructions to a video editor. Included in this material are the raw-footage sheets (everything on the tape), the reporter's script with notations about which shots go where, and any supers or titles that are required. A good reporter always sits down with the editor to answer any questions, to help deal with problems, and to make creative decisions as the story is pieced together. In addition, the reporter will outline the script that the anchor will read to introduce the package.

Interviews

In Chapter 8, we discussed some of the techniques of getting a good interview, but here we should be aware of several considerations particular to television that will make your time in the editing room easier and more productive.

Tip 1. *Start with an establishing shot.* This wide shot will give the audience a sense of where you are and what is going on. It is usually a shot of the interviewer and the subject, with as much background as necessary to identify the locale.

 Tip 2. *Focus your attention on the subject.* The interview is the important thing, and you must concentrate on the person you are speaking to, not the camera, not the crew, not the bystanders. An interviewer who sneaks looks at the producer or camera person is obviously not interested in what the subject is saying, and as a result the person will not be very forthcoming. And an audience can easily see all that eye movement!

 Tip 3. *Most interviews are shot over the interviewer's shoulder.* There is no hard-and-fast rule that this must be so, but it obviously works best, putting the audience in the interviewer's shoes. Avoid standing side by side with the subject, facing the camera.

 Tip 4. *Get several reverse-angle and cutaway shots.* They might be a reporter's reaction shots or repeats of some of the questions that were asked, from the point of view of the subject. They might be footage of the scene or even long shots of the interview, providing visual context. These shots can be used to bridge segments of the subject's conversation, avoiding jump cuts.

 Tip 5. *Get the facts right.* At the end of the interview, have the subject give the spelling and pronunciation of her or his name and full title while the tape is rolling. This is a foolproof reference when you are writing the story back at the studio.

Exercise 21.1

Record a television newscast and transcribe one of the stand-ups. Critique the stand-up, noting especially the following points. Was the reporter's appearance on camera necessary (is there another, better, way that this information could have been conveyed)? Was the background an interesting part of the story? Did reverse-angle shots look natural, as though they were shot by a second camera? Was an establishing shot used?

Exercise 21.2

Record a television newscast and transcribe the packages. List the elements that made up each package (stand-ups, SOT, V/O, interviews) in the order they appeared.

Assignment

Approach a local TV news department and ask if you can accompany one of its ENG crews as an observer for a day. Write a report on the experience, noting the day's events chronologically, the subject of each item shot, the type of coverage (stand-up, package, interview), the crew, and the time spent on each story. Estimate the percentage of time spent on each aspect of a report: planning, writing, shooting, travelling, editing, et cetera.

22

Videography

The videographer or video journalist in today's television news-gathering environment has an interesting and challenging job that combines strong journalistic skills with the ability to produce broadcast-quality video.

The videographer is expected to perform four functions well: producing, shooting, editing, and presenting news stories on a daily basis. Traditionally, these job functions were shared by a producer, camera operator, editor, and reporter. In today's fast-paced, highly competitive television news environment, these tasks are combined to save time and money.

A typical day for a videographer might begin with a meeting during which the news director, producers, reporters, and videographers discuss stories that might be covered for the day's newscasts. All in attendance are expected to contribute ideas for stories. Doing so requires a good knowledge of current issues in the city and surrounding area covered by the television station, an understanding of news values, and a grasp of news-gathering and-writing principles (see Unit One).

The videographer will then shoot the story in an efficient and visually interesting manner, all the while paying attention to content, shot composition, lighting, and sound.

A stand-up is often recorded by the video journalist on location before returning to the station. This means that the videographer has already begun to construct the story on location and has taken into consideration the content of the material that has just been shot. Stand-ups may be designed to open the story, close it, or bridge segments — or to do all three.

Having completed shooting content (interviews, action) and possibly stand-ups at the location of the story, the videographer returns to the station to view and log the material. After viewing and logging the footage, the videographer will write the story and any voice-over narration that is required. If any file footage is needed to tell the story, the videographer will search for it in the station's tape library or archive at this time.

Once the story has been written, the next step is editing. Today's videographer should be a competent operator of both linear, tape-based editing systems and newer computer-based, non-linear editing systems. To edit efficiently and effectively, the videographer must have some understanding of the technical aspects of the television signal and the editing equipment as well as a finely tuned aesthetic sense of picture and sound editing. The story is then edited by the videographer and is sent to the news director for approval before it is aired.

CAREER OPPORTUNITY

Position: Video journalist
Location: News division
Salary: Commensurate with qualifications and experience
Hours of work: 40 hours per week. Shift work and overtime as required.

Responsibilities:
- operates a portable electronic camera and recording unit for field reports to cover items for news and information programming; develops, writes, reports, and edits news stories
- prepares, aligns, sets up, carries, and operates an ENG package and accessories for field reports
- provides creative input to the production of items
- works in conjunction with news production staff and reporters

Qualifications:
- experience with the operation of ENG equipment
- excellent concentration and co-ordination skills
- ability to deal with new and developing technology
- strong on-air presence, ability to craft a story well, and ability to perform in a live environment
- strong people skills and a good understanding of journalistic ethics
- minimum of two years of broadcast experience, preferably in a news environment
- college-level television diploma or equivalent education

At the end of the workday, the typical videographer has created one, possibly even two, complete news stories and may have contributed to another videographer's story by editing it or providing feedback on it.

In some smaller-market stations, the videographer may even be required to anchor the news on occasion and to produce newscasts if the producer is unavailable. This is not an everyday occurrence, but it illustrates both the flexibility required to be a video journalist and the opportunities available to multiskilled individuals.

The Videographer as Producer

In the role of producer, the videographer must be able to find and "pitch" good news items in daily story meetings. You need to know what is going on in your city or town that is newsworthy and how to present a potential story to the station's news director. The real key to success in this role, however, is the ability to get people to talk to you about their stories. Develop a good rapport with a wide range of people, from the average person on the street, to the president of a large organization, to politicians and religious and community leaders.

The videographer/producer must be self-directed. Much freedom comes with a career in videography, but there is an equal amount of responsibility and daily deadline pressure.

The Videographer as Reporter

As a reporter, the videographer must again have excellent interpersonal skills; people should feel comfortable talking to you in front of your camera. It is your job as a reporter to ensure that your subjects want to tell their stories to you and want you to report them. Credibility is a critical factor here. As you begin to report stories in your community, your viewers will form opinions about your qualities as a reporter. They will decide if you are unbiased, fair, and accurate. If you meet these criteria, then you will have credibility with your audience, some of whom will someday be in your reports. One of the challenges in reporting as a videographer is to ensure that you don't "lose the person" because of the equipment you are using. It is the human element of your story that will connect with the audience.

As with producing, reporting also requires the ability to find a story, but more important here is the ability to tell the story. This means asking questions during an interview that will bring out the essence of the story along with its human element (see Unit Three). The reporter must also be able to write and present voice-over narration and on-camera stand-ups with professionalism.

The Videographer as Camera Operator

As the camera operator for your report, you must produce technically correct video that also contains creative pictures. You must be able to use the video camera properly to ensure correct exposure, colour balance, audio level, and time-code generation. The details of these technical settings vary slightly among different makes and models of camera, and are beyond the scope of this book, but you should have a good grasp of camera operation to provide technically acceptable sounds and images. If you learn how to make these adjustments on one type of broadcast camera/recorder (perhaps a Panasonic DVC Pro or a Sony DV Cam) then the adjustments on a Sony Betacam or other unit will be easier for you to make.

Aesthetically pleasing shots require a good eye for composition. Pleasing images often, but not always, make use of certain rules of composition such as "the rule of thirds." In brief, this "law" of photography uses imaginary lines to divide the camera's viewfinder into thirds (like a tick-tack-toe game) and then places the items of most visual significance at the intersection of the lines. Doing so helps to avoid the novice camera operator's common error of centring the subject in the viewfinder; a centred image isn't visually dynamic or interesting. Other considerations when composing a shot include the use of "leading lines," such as railway tracks or other lines to draw the viewer's eye into the shot; the use of sufficient "headroom" above a person being shown on camera; and the use of "lead space" in front of a talking person or a moving person or object.

It is important to vary the type of shot — long shot (LS), medium shot (MS), and close-up (CU) — and to hold the shot long enough to allow you to edit as required. Even experienced camera operators hold each shot for a count of 15 seconds. Considering that the average report on a typical newscast is only 90 seconds, it may seem excessive to hold each shot of action and location for 15 seconds while you shoot it, but doing so ensures that you will have enough material during editing.

The steadiness of each shot is also important. For this reason, a tripod is extremely useful to a videographer; in fact, it's a necessity for shooting a stand-up, since the reporter and camera operator are the same person! Most serious interviews and standard shots will look better if the camera is stable, but some fast-breaking news situations won't allow the time required to set up a tripod. These situations call for a steady over-the-shoulder hand-held technique, which requires much practice. The novice videographer or student of videography would be wise to use a tripod when possible and to practise and perfect a stable hand-held shooting technique.

Certain situations will look better if shot with camera movement. The key here is to ensure that there is always a motivation for the movement. Ask yourself why you would want to move the camera, and then move it only when there is a really good reason for doing so, such as panning to follow movement by the subject or tilting to capture the top of a burning building as well as the firefighters on the street below. It is wise to shoot a static version of a moving shot to ensure that you always have a steady image in editing if you need it. As you gain experience, or if a certain style is desired by the station you work for, adjustments to your technique can be made.

Lighting is another area of concern for the videographer as camera operator. The most common form of portable lighting is a small battery-operated light mounted directly on top of the camera. Although it provides sufficient illumination for a nearby subject, it results in a flat or two-dimensional image. A direct light of this type tends to be harsh, producing deep shadows. To achieve a more pleasing effect, camera operators often add a layer of diffusion material to soften the light and then tilt it upward to feather it so that there will be some variation in the intensity of light reaching the subject.

The other source of light is existing light. The key here is to ensure that you have correctly white-balanced the camera for the situation. Take advantage of the direction of existing light; as a general rule, do not shoot into a strong light source such as the sun or a window or a powerful indoor light. Rather, position your camera so that the light source is behind you and the camera and is illuminating your subject.

In essence, the role of the videographer as camera operator is to provide a variety of stable, correctly lit, sharply focussed shots that are held long enough to allow choices in editing.

The Videographer as Sound Recordist

It is equally important to ensure that any sound being recorded is very clear. To achieve this goal, the videographer must use the correct type of microphone for the situation: a hand-held or lapel microphone for interviews and perhaps the on-camera microphone for location sound. Recording sound at the correct level is also extremely important. This level may vary somewhat with the make and model of equipment, but avoid using any type of "automatic gain control" and instead adjust your audio levels manually. Always use headphones to monitor sound clarity as well as listen for loud background noises or any buzzes or hums that may be caused by a poorly connected microphone. When doing your own stand-ups, you should play back your tape right after recording and listen carefully to the sound to evaluate its quality.

The Videographer as Writer

As a writer, the videographer must be able to organize 15 to 20 minutes of video footage into a coherent, concise, and interesting (possibly even entertaining) 90-second story. Voice-over narration must be written to complete the story and to link the elements into a cohesive whole. An introduction for the anchor must be considered. All the elements of good reporting and writing come into play to pull together the stand-ups, the interviews, the establishing shots, the action footage, and the cutaways into a polished story.

The Videographer as Editor

The ability to tell a story using sound and moving pictures is the primary function of the television editor. The first step is often the production of a shot log that lists all the shots and where on the tape they are located. Next the editor begins to build the story from the footage according to the script. The videographer must know when to cut, which shots can be effectively spliced together, how long to hold a shot, and all the other principles of effective video editing. A news editor should be able to edit using both tape-based linear editing systems and computer-based non-linear editing systems. These techniques and technologies are well beyond the scope of this text, but the videographer as editor needs to be familiar with them.

Conclusion

Overall, the videographer or video journalist must have some technical understanding of cameras, recorders, microphones, shooting and editing techniques and equipment, and major news-gathering tape formats, such as Betacam and DVC PRO. By being familiar with the technical workings of the equipment you are using, you will be able to operate it properly and efficiently and troubleshoot problems that may occur in the field. Spend as much time with as many different types of equipment as you can.

While the videographer must master a great deal of technology, it should be transparent to the audience. This is an important point: you have to master the tools, but the audience is really only interested in the story, not in the equipment and techniques that you have used to get it. Strong reporting and writing skills are at the heart of videography. No matter how well shot, recorded, lit, and edited a piece is, it is only as strong as the storytelling that makes it affect an audience.

Exercise 22.1

Record a news report of 60 to 90 seconds. Create a shot log and a script that describes each shot used in the report and the verbal content that accompanies that shot. Time the length of each shot and note the type of shot and the position of the camera. Look for the use of compositional rules. Were any of the rules broken? Examine the flow of the report in terms of the transition from one image to the next. How well does the story "flow" from shot to shot? Try to determine how the videographer approached the visuals used to tell the story.

Exercise 22.2

Shoot some footage of a person interacting with an object such as a computer. How many different shot types and camera positions can you use to tell this simple visual story? Consider using several different shots: an establishing shot, a medium shot taken over the subject's shoulder, a close-up of the subject's hands on the keyboard, and a medium shot and a close-up of the screen. Then shoot a reverse-angle shot from behind the computer (looking over the computer's "shoulder"), then a medium shot and a close-up of the subject's head and face. This may seem like a lot of shooting, but it will give you many options in editing. This approach to shooting an interaction can be applied to many types of person-to-object or person-to-person situations.

In the editing suite, create two versions, one 15 seconds long and one ten seconds long.

Exercise 22.3

Shoot an interview with a friend using a small camera-mounted light. Experiment with the use of diffusion in front of the light and with the angle of the light on the subject to produce a pleasing image. If your light has a dichroic filter, experiment with it as well to determine how effective it is when used under outdoor lighting conditions. Try using the camera light out of doors without white-balancing the camera for outdoor light. Make use of existing light outdoors and indoors. How can you use natural light to create pleasing images quickly?

Assignment

In the course of one day, find a local newsworthy event and produce a complete report on it of 60 to 90 seconds. Doing so will give you a sense of the amount of work and the amount of time that a videographer expends to produce a report for the nightly news. Compare your report with the reports you see on television. Ask yourself if this is something you could do every day. How and where can you improve? Is your work stronger or weaker than what you see on the news? How and why? What will you change in your approach for the next story you cover?

23

The Television Newscast

The Lineup

We have already discussed news values and radio newscast lineup; now might be a good time to review that chapter before we begin examining the television newscast in more detail. News values such as proximity, immediacy, human interest, and the availability and quality of tape are used (instinctively by most experienced newspeople) to assess the newsworthiness of the stories that might become part of the newscast. When those stories are being assembled into the lineup, the over-riding rule is that the best stories go first, and those with progressively less news value show up later in the program. This pattern is very flexible, though, and the placement of stories in the lineup is also influenced by factors such as grouping stories that are alike in some way (theme, location) or by station policy, which may require a specific pattern for the stories in the newscast.

In discussing the lineup considerations for television, we can fine-tune these factors and look in detail at how a newscast is constructed. While radio news is not immune to the amount of thought and effort that goes into arranging the order of stories in a TV newscast, it is unusual for a radio newscast to go through the intense scrutiny that a TV lineup is subjected to (an exception is CBC Radio's half-hour network newscast *The World at Six*). While radio provides news hourly (more or less, depending on the station), TV newscasts are less frequent, much longer, and therefore given much more significance: a radio newscast is ordinarily the work of one or two people, while a TV newscast might take 20, even at a small station.

NEWS VALUES

First, our consideration of news values is modified by the nature of the TV program. Most stations are part of a national or regional network, and the local newscast is run in tandem with the network's newscast. Since the network covers the big national and international events, proximity becomes hugely important for the local newscast. Even stations that do not belong to a network emphasize local events, since they recognize that people tune in to them, instead of the networks, to get community content. All of the other news values are skewed to allow for this emphasis on proximity.

News values are also modified by the time of day of the newscast. Audiences change over the course of a day, and a morning newscast must cater to those who went to bed early and want a summary of what happened during late evening and overnight. Sports, especially, have a major role in the morning newscast, which updates the late-night scores and results. At mid-day, the news must be tailored to fit the stay-at-home person who probably has heard at least one newscast and is aware of the day's major stories. What is this person interested in? How can the newscast be modified to appeal to the demographic that is tuned in? The evening newscast is similarly adapted to cater to the needs of an audience that is presumably interested in being updated about all the newsworthy events of the day.

FLOW AND PACE

Second, there is a great deal of emphasis in TV news on "flow" and "pace." While the grouping of stories with similar themes and content will produce a unified flow in the newscast, especially when the stories are linked together with transitions (see "Tosses" below), how do you get flow in a program that is interrupted by commercials and breaks for weather, sports, and perhaps business, entertainment, and agricultural reports? Flow is accomplished by carefully and creatively assembling the newscast so that each segment (section of the newscast separated from the others by commercials) has its own flow. Instead of simply putting the best story first, the least newsworthy last, and arranging the others in between, the good news producer will try to insert a good story after each break, to lead each segment of the newscast. Furthermore, "Teasers" (see below) will be inserted just before commercials to add flow and to tempt the audience to wait out the advertisements to see the next segment.

This arrangement also helps to maintain pace. The audience must never be given the opportunity to become uninterested, and several techniques are used to make sure viewers stay tuned in. One is the use of a strong story to lead each segment. Another is to arrange stories so that there is variety in the presentation. Three or four stand-ups in a row or three or four readers one after the other will cause boredom, killing the pace of the show. Thus, the lineup will be juggled to ensure that there is an interesting mix of packages, stand-ups, and readers: a variety of images on the screen from "talking head" to SOT, from analysis to action. One might argue that entertainment values are replacing solid, serious, journalistic values here, but few news producers even stop to consider the matter in putting together a package that will not only inform but also grab and hold an audience.

Posting date:
Position: Newswriter/lineup editor
Location:
Salary: Commensurate with qualifications and experience
Hours of work: 40 hours per week. Variable shifts.

Description: Contribute to news programs by writing scripts for on-camera, voice over, and intros. Line up news two shifts per week. Supervise editing of videotape for reports and voice-over packages, vet reporters' scripts, and advise on aspects of reports. Other duties as assigned.

Essential qualifications:
- excellent knowledge of domestic and international news and current affairs
- experience in broadcast writing
- proven ability to meet deadlines
- ability to work in a team
- self-motivated and composed under pressure
- good computer skills
- excellent written and oral communications

Desirable qualifications:
- broadcast or journalism degree
- French or other language skills

TIMING

The length of a news program is decided by the station, and, because it must fit in with the rest of the daily schedule, that program can't be extended if there is a lot of news to communicate on a certain day or shortened if it's been a slow day. One of the producer's biggest challenges is to fit the news that is available into the precise number of minutes and seconds of the schedule. In a 30-minute local newscast, there will be four or five minutes of commercials, four or five minutes of sports, about three minutes of weather, a minute for an intro and extro, plus teases, tosses, and interaction among the anchors — leaving about 15 minutes for news. If you figure that an average story will run two minutes, your newscast consists of seven or eight stories. Each reporter who has covered something that day will push for her or his story, trying to make the case not just that it be included but also that it be given more time and a better position in the lineup. If a reporter has been out covering a story, then the story should be aired, because not to do so would mean that the resources of the station (reporter's, crew's, and editor's time, equipment, vehicles, etc.) have been wasted.

The news producer's responsibility, then, is to assemble a newscast that is faithful to news values, fulfils the audience's needs and wants, flows, has pace and variety, uses all the material provided by the station's reporters, and comes out on time to the second! It is a tough job. It is accomplished by fitting the pieces together like a carpenter, cutting here, chopping there, rounding this off so it fits better with that, and using some filler where necessary.

The buffers that can be expanded or contracted a little to make the other parts fit are the weather and, to a lesser degree, sports. In addition, anchors can be given one or two short marginal items to read if time needs to be filled, and the time spent in ad-libbed conversation on the set can be lengthened or shortened. Often a feature story will be designated to end the newscast and then "backtimed" so that the director knows exactly when it must begin in order for it to end at the last second of the program. The other stories are then fitted in before that feature.

The Lineup Sheet

Many stations have variations on the lineup sheet to meet the individual needs of their crews and equipment, though many are now being standardized by computer programs that assist the editor in piecing together a newscast. The one below is quite simple and straightforward, providing the entire crew with clear information: page number of the story, which anchor is on camera, story slug, video, time of the item, and a running total of the time of the newscast.

PG	TLNT	SLUG	VIDEO	TIME	TRT
A1	M/C	OPEN	LIVE	0:30	0:30
A2	MIKE	FATAL CRASH	ESS/LIVE	1:20	1:50
A3	CRIS	FIRE UPDATE	ESS/VTR	2:04	3:54
A4	MIKE	COUNCIL DEBATE	CG/VTR	2:20	6:14
A5	M/C	TEASE AWARD	LIVE	0:15	6:29
—	BREAK 1	————	BREAK	2:00	8:29
B1	CRIS	CANADA AWARD	CG/VTR	1:22	9:51
B2	MIKE	SCHOOL EXAMS	VTR	2:32	12:23
B3	MIKE	UNEMPLOYMENT	ESS/LIVE	0:35	12:58
B4	CRIS	STORE OPENING	VTR V/O	0:55	13:53
B5	CRIS	KID FINDER	ESS/LIVE	0:40	14:33
B6	M/C	TEASE WEATHER	LIVE	0:15	14:48
—	BREAK 2	————	BREAK	2:00	16:48
C1	PHIL	WEATHER	LIVE	3:30	20:18
C2	M/C	TEASE SPORTS	LIVE	0:10	20:28
—	BREAK 3	————	BREAK	1:00	21:28
D1	VAL	INTRO	LIVE	0:20	21:48
D2	VAL	BOAR HOCKEY	VTR V/O	1:46	23:34
D3	VAL	GOLF REPORT	VTR V/O	2:10	25:44
D4	VAL	SCORE SUMMARY	CG V/O	0:35	26:19
D5	VAL	TEASE KICKER	LIVE	0:15	26:34
—	BREAK 4	————	BREAK	2:00	28:34
E1	M/C	SENIORS DANCE	VTR V/O	1:20	29:54
E2	ALL	EXTRO	LIVE	0:06	30:00

Such a lineup sheet can do no more than give an approximation of what is happening, but it keeps everyone in the crew up to date on what should happen, how long it should take, and who is responsible for it. Some line-up sheets include a column for SOURCE to indicate where the video signal is coming from, and many have a section for AUDIO source; some have a separate column for graphics (GFX), and others include a column for the writer's name. The video column could include the type of live shot required (a two-shot, e.g., when the anchors are tossing an item or conversing). By the time the program is over, the lineup sheet has been marked up and written over as items have been added or deleted and decisions have been made at the last minute.

Exercise 23.1

Record a local TV newscast and fill in a lineup sheet modelled on the one above to reflect what happened during the program. You'll need a stopwatch.

Teases, Tosses, and Kickers

A tease or teaser is a short preview of an upcoming story. Some teasers use video footage and anchor V/O, while others are simply readers. A good teaser will capture interest and make the viewer want to know the details of the story, so it must not reveal too much. On the other hand, it should not set up expectations of sensational or dramatic content that are not met. You may trick an audience into watching something this way once, but they won't believe a teaser a second time. The video that is selected to go with a V/O teaser should similarly attract interest without giving away your best footage.

When using two anchors, transitions between stories can be accomplished by using a toss, a line that leads from the story just finished directly into the story that the other anchor is about to introduce. Tosses are also used when several reporters are covering different aspects of the same story. At the end of one package, the reporter will conclude the stand-up by tossing to the next reporter's package.

> PAT: This forest fire is a long way from being under control, and without some help from the weatherman we could have more evacuations, more loss of property. Dan diBuono has the latest from the weather office and the prospects for relief.
>
> DAN: Head meteorologist Kevin Grossman has his fingers crossed like all of us, but he has the expertise and the equipment to. . . .

A kicker is a light, often humorous, story used to end a newscast or a segment on an upbeat note. Keep in mind when selecting kickers that not everyone shares the same sense of humour, and be sensitive to the fact that much of the newscast may have had tragic elements; a kicker that makes light of someone's problems or ridicules a person might trigger a nasty audience response.

Exercise 23.2

Repeat Exercise 23.1 with a different station. This is an excellent way to get a feel for the complexity of lining up a newscast, juggling news values, pace, flow, and making the whole thing come out exactly on time.

Exercise 23.3

1. You are the producer of a half-hour newscast and have selected the following stories for this evening's news. There are three commercial breaks of two minutes each, one at approximately six minutes into the package, one at about 16 minutes, and the last at roughly 24 minutes (some flexibility is possible, but commercials must appear no more than a minute from their scheduled positions). Sports is normally between three and four minutes, weather about two to three minutes, and there is a packaged agriculture report that runs 1:30 and must be included. Arrange your stories around these elements to produce a workable lineup sheet.

   - Stand-up: 3:30 — Yesterday's devastating hailstorm has farmers adding up their losses . . . some lost their entire crops. Estimates of total damage are in the 12-million-dollar range.
   - Stand-up: 2:50 — Food poisoning is being given as the cause of a mysterious illness that affected 33 students at Vincent Massey High School today. Fears of a contagious disease were put to rest, and food services personnel in the high school cafeteria are checking.
   - Reader: 1:40 — Union workers at Dreesling Fine Foods have elected a new president for their local. She's Vivian Crow, who has been with the company for 14 years in the food-processing department and was vice-president of the union. She replaces Kevin Hvilivitski, who retired after two terms as president.
   - Reader: 1:10 — City police are at the scene of a serious three-vehicle collision on the Centre Street bridge. Several ambulances and emergency vehicles are also standing by . . . no details yet about injuries.
   - Package: 4:10 — New provincial guidelines will mean stronger emphasis on so-called basics at primary schools and less time for other activities. Some local parents, teachers, and students favour the changes, but others aren't so sure.
   - Package: 2:15 — City council last night heard from three groups hoping to get grants from the city treasury. All made presentations, but a decision was referred to committee for recommendations and will be brought forward at next month's council meeting.

2. Write teasers to be read just before each of the commercial breaks. The teasers can be used to assist in filling time but must be carefully written to fit the space available.

Answers to Selected Exercises

Chapter 1: What Is News? (pages 5 to 12)

Exercise 1.2

1. Many variations are possible, depending on previous newscasts, the immediacy of the events, the importance of the events to the local community, and so on. One likely arrangement is 2, 6, 4, 7, 3, 5, 1. This lineup assumes that the picket line violence is the top story, then puts the two firefighter stories together, followed by another local event (the mayor is running again). Provincial, national, and international stories follow in that order; proximity is the guide since none of them is dramatically more newsworthy than another. Another arrangement would have the fire story first, followed by the settlement of the firefighters' wage dispute, followed by another union story (the violence on the picket line).

2. The most likely lead story is the gas leak (it has proximity, impact, and immediacy), followed by the accident. The peacekeepers and the tank purchase should be linked either before or after the land claim settlement (depending on location and audience interest in Aboriginal affairs). The two disaster stories (earthquake and hurricane) are also linked, with the Florida one getting priority because of possible impact (vacationers). 5, 3, 7, 2, 1, 4, 6, 8.

3. The layoff of city workers/no tax hike story has impact and proximity in an otherwise unspectacular news lineup. The vandalism story is also local and might be balanced by the journalism award. The good news for Ford is variable depending on its impact on the local community. B.C. protesters should be linked with the rain forest story, and the international trade story should be last. 6, 4, 2, 7, 5, 1, 3.

Chapter 3: "Telling" the News (pages 18 to 27)

Exercise 3.1

1 With fewer than half the eligible voters casting a ballot, Miriam Saguchi won easily, collecting more than 50 percent of the vote. Vernon Clarke placed second, and Wendy Grumann was third.

2. This month's annual inflation rate is just over two percent, down a little from last month, and over half a percent lower than a year ago. High interest rates of almost five percent are being given credit for the decline.

3. A huge new warehouse is to be built at the corner of Station Street and First Avenue. Fantastic Products Company president Sheila Moffatt made the announcement today.

4. The thief escaped out the back door and got away in a silver luxury car driven by a partner.

5. An unexplained explosion at the chemical plant this morning is the cause of the fire and the cloud of oily, black smoke over the city.

Exercise 3.2

1. The satellite erected a sun screen to protect it from the intense rays of the sun in outer space.

2. After taking second, Chavez, the Cincinnati shortstop, hardly paused before stealing third.

3. A snow squall is blamed for a pileup on the Trans-Canada at Ninth Street that sent four people to hospital this morning. Two are reported to have been hurt seriously. That's the same stretch of road where a 50-car accident caused several deaths last year. Today's storm reduced visibility to near zero and caused some sections of the highway to ice up.

4. The Grape and Wine Festival Parade took over Saint Paul Street in Saint Catharines today. It was a day to celebrate one of the largest harvests in recent years.

5. A hidden tape recorder was used to collect the evidence.

Exercise 3.3

1. City council members voted 12 to seven in favour of giving themselves their first raise in five years last night. Over the two years of the new deal, they will get a 14 percent raise, bringing a councillor's annual salary up to 24 thousand, 300 dollars.

2. The deal to bring a ten-storey hotel complex to the downtown core has now been signed. Hi-Rise Developments of Edmonton will spend over 160 million dollars on the project, which is expected to create about two thousand construction jobs. The complex will be built in two phases, beginning next month. The hotel is scheduled to be finished by spring of next year and the shopping plaza, parking, and conference facilities a year later. When it's all completed, the plans call for more than 300 full-time jobs to result.

3. Designated stores in tourist areas will soon be able to sell Canadian wines over the counter. The government official who made the announcement this morning says that the necessary legislation will be introduced in the winter. However, she cautioned that this is an attempt to promote Canadian wines, and the stores and their locations will be strictly regulated to prevent competition with the Liquor Control Board.

4. Last year's rookie driver of the year is leaving the local track to compete internationally. Dennis Mason will be moving up to the NASCAR circuit next year in a new car built in Winnipeg. Mason is the current points leader in this year's Man-

itoba Driver's Championship, and last month's Merritville Speedway Challenge Cup. The new car will be sponsored by Corntech Racing and built on a Ford frame by Mason's crew. They hope to have it ready and tested in time for next year's racing season.

5. According to the government's own figures, Canadians have a higher tax burden than any other industrialized country but one. The total of all taxes paid by Canadians has climbed to almost 40 percent of the gross domestic product. Only France, with a tax burden of about 44 percent, is higher among the seven major industrial democracies.

Chapter 4: Broadcast Writing Conventions (pages 31 to 41)

Exercise 4.1
1. Four million, 567 thousand, 909 dollars
2. 7 this evening
3. 794 point five (or 794 and a half)
4. four dollars and 95 cents
5. nine percent
6. eleven million, 565 thousand
7. 371
8. seven and three-quarters
9. one hundred and eleven point nine
10. 604 thousand, 411 dollars, and four cents

Exercise 4.2
1. Saint John's Mayor Kevin Murphy has worked for Sysco Limited since 1992.
2. Canada was a charter member of NATO and has more recently joined the Organization of American States.
3. The wanted man fled Saint Thomas, Ontario, and was later seen in Port Alberni, B-C, where he was picked up by the R-C-M-P.
4. The U-S is trying to get an agreement on agriculture at the General Agreement on Tariffs and Trade [or GATT since it has become a reasonably well-known acronym] talks in Saint John's, Newfoundland.
5. The Canadian Radio-Television and Telecommunications Commission has granted an extension to the licence of the C-B-C. [Another way to handle this one that avoids the awkwardness of the long title would be to begin "Canada's communications watchdog, the C-R-T-C, has granted. . . ."]
6. A report from the Canadian Security and Intelligence Service says that the governor general of Canada and the lieutenant governor of Alberta were under surveillance by the C-I-A during a period in the mid-1960s.
7. The United Autoworkers union and the N-D-P have different views on how to handle the question of layoffs at G-M in Saint Catharines, Ontario.
8. Three people have been rushed to Colson Memorial Hospital after a three-car collision on Windsor Avenue at Dawson Drive this morning.
9. Northwest winds of 30 kilometres per hour will swing to the northeast and pick up 12 or 15 kilometres in strength by this afternoon.

10. General Mackenzie and Lieutenant White will speak at the Canadian Association of Broadcasters convention in Fort Lauderdale, Florida, about the media's role in U-N peacekeeping operations.

Exercise 4.3
 1. Patrick Roy [roo-wha]
 2. Michael Ondaatje [on DA chay]
 3. Sarajevo [sara YAY vo]
 4. Antonio Vivaldi [vi VAL dee]
 5. Galapagos [gal LA pagos] Islands

Exercise 4.5
 1. The new mayor is Cynthia Boyko, who has served on city council for seven years, representing the Broadway Drive and Clager Street district.
 2. A member of the provincial task force studying the problem of violence against women says that it's a problem that must be solved by men. Mary Gallagher was speaking. . . .
 3. Northern Industries Limited says that its profits fell by half a percent last year, resulting in the planned layoffs.
 4. Officers from the M-N-R [or Ministry of Natural Resources, depending on the familiarity of your audience with those initials; an urban audience would likely need it written out, while a rural — especially a northern — audience would not] were called in to check the animal for rabies after it had attacked John Spodafori [spoda FOR ee].
 5. The Saskatchewan minister of agriculture says that Canada must stand up to the Europeans in order to preserve our supply management system of agricultural marketing.
 6. The village treasurer says the new three point six percent tax increase will raise over 45 thousand dollars, which will cut into last year's budget deficit.
 7. The Stallions . . . in the playoffs for the first time in six years . . . need a good performance from their rookie goaltender, Marc Dupuis [doo PWEE].
 8. A county meeting of the Parent–Teacher Association at 6 tonight will debate the "half week" proposal suggested by the teachers' union.
 9. According to police, a man flashing a hunting knife entered the convenience store on Saint James Avenue at around 6 this morning and demanded money.
10. The federal government is increasing the amount paid in transfer fees to the provinces, and that's good news for P-E-I's finance minister, Wilson Deng.

Exercise 4.6
 1. A local man is under arrest following a high-speed chase along Niagara Street and Highway 145 early this morning. In custody is Fredrick Schleich of Dundas Avenue.
 2. A blind eight-year-old refugee will soon get a seeing-eye dog, thanks to the efforts of the local Lions Club. In just over six weeks, it raised 12 thousand 500 dollars to help Tabatha Moullambasi [mool am BAZE ee], who was blinded by a bullet during the war in her native Somalia.

3. The 38 members of the city's Youth Orchestra will be travelling to Saint Peters-burg, Russia, this summer. The young people . . . aged nine to 21 . . . received a grant from Telecomp Incorporated to make the trip possible.

4. Following a facelift operation that he says was botched, a local man is suing his doctor for a million dollars. Ted Dykstra claims that, following the operation, his facial skin is so tight he can't close his eyes. Doctor Renatta Yager performed the operation on Dykstra three months ago.

5. An early morning accident on Harwell Street has resulted in the deaths of two local people. Judith and Kevin Ryker were killed, and their seven-year-old daugh-ter Cindy is in County General Hospital with serious injuries. The two occupants of the other car were also seriously hurt. They are from Miami, Florida.

Chapter 5: The Lead (pages 42 to 51)

Exercise 5.1
1. The eight astronauts who flew the space shuttle *Pegasus* are back safely after ten days in space.
2. After six months of duty in the Middle East, 50 Canadian peacekeepers are home.
3. The government is making 50 million dollars available to help young people get their first jobs.
4. Four people are dead, including a Canadian, and two are still missing after an avalanche in the Swiss Alps.
5. Mayor Diane Lewicki is the Liberal candidate for April's by-election.

Exercise 5.2
1. A Speelton woman has been killed in a car accident.
2. A teacher at Confederation High School has won a marathon race in Japan.
3. Aid workers in Somalia have received a shipment of medical supplies and food.
4. Retailers have had the best Christmas in ten years, according to the Better Busi-ness Bureau.
5. Parliament has adjourned for the summer recess with several issues unresolved.

Exercise 5.3
1. A local teenager has been badly hurt in a knifing incident outside a Main Street bar.
2. After almost 14 hours of negotiations, city workers have been offered a three-year contract.
3. The city streets are clear of last night's 30-centimetre snowfall, just in time for rush hour.
4. A local woman is the proud mother of quadruplets this morning.
5. Many city residents are a little tired this morning, but no injuries or damage has been reported after last night's earthquake.
6. About 40 people are dead and 20 missing after a ferry capsized yesterday in Panama.
7. A High Street family owe their lives to an alert guard dog this morning.

8. A local priest whose work in the community has made him a popular figure is dead.
9. Workers at the Tinman Foundry are out on strike.
10. The police budget is one of the victims of last night's Financial Committee meeting.

Exercise 5.4
1. A Canadian wine company has won a gold medal at a competition in France.
2. Molson's and Labatt's are still Canada's biggest brewers, sharing about 93 percent of the beer market.
3. The head of a school board in southern Alberta says that teachers are overpaid and underworked.
4. A hit-and-run accident this morning has left a woman in serious condition in hospital.
5. Two people are under arrest following a scuffle on the picket line at Memorial Enterprises this morning.
6. Hurricane Dennis is now battering North Carolina after causing four deaths and more than ten million dollars of damage in South Carolina.
7. A measure to reduce the number of councillors comes before town council tonight.
8. Mayor Trillman says he's just fine after his triple by-pass surgery this morning.
9. Two boys . . . missing in the woods north of Clearwater for three days . . . are safe and unharmed.
10. A Windsor man is facing sexual assault charges after a three-week police investigation.

Exercise 5.5
1. The price of that morning cup of coffee is about to rise.
2. A man convicted of nine robberies is going to jail for two years.
3. A rookie city councillor is unhappy about the city's budget process.
4. Three people are dead after an early morning collision on Highway 18.
5. A local company is going to supply shoes to the Canadian army, and 20 new jobs will result.

Chapter 6: Building the Story (pages 52 to 56)

Exercise 6.1
A three-alarm fire is burning out of control this morning on Purvis Avenue. When firefighters responded to the call at 6 this morning, they found the house already burning furiously. As a precaution, the houses to either side of the burning home have been evacuated. The family of four who live in the house are reported safe, but one firefighter has been sent to hospital with a suspected broken foot.

Exercise 6.2
A city councillor has been charged with assault and resisting arrest during an incident at today's Gay Pride Day parade. Howard Gleason led the fight against approval for the parade during the heated city council debate two months ago. He and two

others were arrested after insults were shouted at parade marchers and a fight broke out. The parade attracted about two thousand marchers, including floats and bands, and an estimated four to five thousand onlookers. Organizers are calling the Gay Pride Day march a huge success in spite of the scuffle.

Chapter 7: Broadcast Style (pages 57 to 68)

Exercise 7.1
1. Many Legion members were angry about the decision to allow hats to be worn in the building.
2. A fire . . . caused by a train derailment near Red Deer . . . is still not under control.
3. The cost of employment insurance will rise tomorrow because the fund is 600 billion dollars in debt.
4. Doctors at the local hospital are hoping to get new equipment that will help them to detect cancer sooner in some cases.
5. Clorisco Industries will soon be laying off about 34 of its workers.
6. According to the lawyer for the convicted man, an appeal is likely.
7. A neighbour of the dead man said that she heard a fight between him and another man just before the accident.
8. Good news for customers of the Downtown Shopping Centre. It will be staying open until 10 at night this month.
9. City police officers will be getting new guns. A decision last night by the police board has authorized the use of semi-automatics.
10. The school will build two ramps to obey new provincial rules that say all public buildings have to be wheelchair accessible.

Exercise 7.2
1. The price increase of <u>only</u> three dollars per ticket was announced today by the team owners.
2. A crowd of <u>fewer than ten thousand</u> <u>showed up</u> at Parliament Hill to protest the controversial proposal.
3. The fundraiser pulled in <u>just</u> three thousand dollars, <u>but</u> organizers said they were pleased.
4. Police in Manitoba have <u>finally</u> captured an escaped convict who has been on the loose since Wednesday.
5. The mayor <u>insisted</u> that the restructuring proposal will increase efficiency in the county clerk's office.
6. Developers estimate that about 200 new jobs will be created if their <u>innovative</u> plan is allowed to proceed.
7. Gerry Mason was attacked by a <u>vicious</u> dog as he innocently walked along Water Street at about 3:30 this morning.
8. The teenager was hit by a car as he <u>staggered</u> across MacLeod Road.
9. When the <u>pretty</u> 25-year-old was appointed to the position, she became the youngest city clerk in the 150-year history of the municipality.
10. The students <u>fortunately</u> called off their walkout when the administration <u>threatened</u> to take legal action.

Exercise 7.3
1. until family have been told
2. the robber (killer, mugger) ran away
3. the building was destroyed by the four-alarm fire
4. police searched the neighbourhood for the missing child
5. the number of people killed in traffic accidents this weekend

Exercise 7.4
1. It is not yet certain that the old way of doing things is best for this council.
2. The fast early pace may tire the leaders.
3. Mayor Williams was very clear in telling the council forcefully that he thought their proposal was unacceptable.
4. Police investigators haven't yet figured out the amount of the damage.
5. The explosions of a dawn artillery barrage ended the silence.

Exercise 7.5
1. There aren't many politicians whose private lives can stand up to the kind of examination sometimes conducted by the media.
2. It isn't your fault that the client didn't choose our design for his stationery.
3. A nice Jaguar in silver blue would be the perfect complement for your new jeans.
4. The counsel he gave you should lead to peace of mind and higher morale.
5. She'd rather go where there is peace and quiet than to a crowded mall.
6. If I take your advice, I'll lose my personal savings.
7. The effect of too much dining out is that you have to lose weight.
8. How does a person whose conscience bothers him ever do anything that conflicts with his principles?
9. It's later than we thought, so we'll have to eat dessert and leave.
10. A course in etiquette would teach you to avoid coarse language and to accept compliments gracefully.

Exercise 7.6
1. Stevens hit the ball down the left-field line and into the seats for a ground-rule double.
2. Farmers who are afraid of losing their government subsidies demonstrated in France today.
3. The provincial legislature has passed a law that will force large corporations to pay a minimum tax.
4. More than 40 thousand fans watched the victory parade as it wound through downtown.
5. Private investigators have located a man whose distant relative left him more than four million dollars.

Exercise 7.7
1. Police are requesting anyone who might have seen something that evening to call the emergency hotline.
2. The number of people who are out of work has fallen for the third consecutive month.

3. Parade organizers awarded the best float a large trophy, which they had found in the basement of City Hall.
4. Sommers told the winner . . . Gionelli . . . that he had beaten him fairly.
5. The committee . . . in presenting its financial statement . . . accused city council of failing to account for its expenditures.

Exercise 7.8
1. Police officers brought the accused men into the heavily guarded courtroom handcuffed together and wearing leg irons.
2. The United Way collected almost 30 thousand dollars in the first week of the spring fundraising campaign.
3. Taxes will rise nearly seven percent next year.
4. An emergency crew rescued the driver after he had swerved off the road and was trapped in his wrecked car.
5. The judge fined the convicted man ten thousand dollars in addition to the sentence of almost 30 years in jail.

Exercise 7.9
1. Cloud seeding to enhance rainfall and prevent snowstorms was expected to be a breakthrough in weather control.
2. The bizarre lives of many rock stars captivate the attention of young fans.
3. Everybody we see at the wrestling matches cheers for The Mad Austrian.
4. Many cities in Russia have a "kremlin" because the word simply signifies a fortress or citadel.
5. The rate of business bankruptcies is rising monthly.
6. All of us at the college feel that cheating and plagiarism are a serious offence.
7. The variety of Richard's money-making activities is amazing: he plays cards, bets on horses, and sells stocks.
8. One can't help noticing that the orchestra is playing better now that the conductor is sober.
9. At lunch time, our cafeteria, with its dreary salad bar, greasy chips, and soggy burgers, takes away my appetite.
10. The reason for Canada's success in the downhill races was many years of hard work on the part of our skiers.

Chapter 9: Reporting Basics (pages 84 to 92)

Exercise 9.1
1. A light truck hit Harriet Trevain as she was crossing the street. Jane Sutherland has been charged with careless driving.
2. OK
3. OK
4. Following the incident, Renatta Scarlatti was charged by police with impaired driving and driving while her licence was under suspension.
5. According to witnesses, a man entered the store and pointed a gun at the cashier. When he had all the money, the thief ran from the store and jumped into a black car driven by another man.

Chapter 11: Rewriting (pages 98 to 106)

Exercise 11.1

1. The lead in this story is the recapture of the two men and might be written in several ways to prevent repetition. "Two escaped prisoners are back in Midvale this morning after a few hours of freedom." "A prison break at Midvale is over." The other facts in the story could be presented in almost any order in the two stories.

2. The evacuation of Riverside is the lead and might be revised in many ways. "The town of Riverside has been evacuated in case the hydro dam on the Little Crow Creek collapses." "The hydro dam on Little Crow Creek is threatened by floodwaters, and the town of Riverside has been evacuated." The two deaths should be reported early in the story, and the forecast is naturally suited to the end.

3. The lead should be about the record, with various details to follow. The name of the boat, the lure, the son's name, where they had it photographed — all are details that might appear in one story but not in another for the sake of variety. "A record-sized sunfish has been pulled from the waters of Halibut Lake." "For the first time in 30 years, Daryl Dalrymple decided to go fishing, and he landed a possible world record."

Exercise 11.2

1. A new study shows that early detection is the key to beating rheumatoid arthritis. Researchers discovered that, if sufferers were given a series of anti-rheumatic drugs within the first five years of being diagnosed, they had the greatest improvement.

2. Germany's tighter immigration laws are being cited as the cause of a drop in the number of people seeking asylum there. According to the Interior Ministry, last year over 300 thousand people claimed asylum in Germany, a decrease from the year before.

3. The woman charged with kidnapping a Burlington baby is wanted in two American states. Baby Shelby Walsh was taken from a Burlington hospital two weeks ago by a woman posing as a hospital worker but was recovered unharmed eleven hours later. Police now say that the woman in custody and accused of the kidnapping is also wanted in Oklahoma and Michigan.

4. A heart attack victim owes his life to the training of an R-C-M-P officer this morning. Gerard Lavoie collapsed while shopping in the Parkview Mall. Former Mountie Howard Schmidt happened to be nearby and applied lifesaving techniques to revive Lavoie, who is now in satisfactory condition in Saint Joseph's hospital. Sergeant Schmidt, who retired from the force two years ago, says this is the first time in 26 years that he has used his C-P-R training.

5. The heavy storm that hit the central and northeastern United States has left transportation in a shambles. Airports from Pittsburgh to Boston are closed or operating on reduced schedules. Interstate highways have been closed by ice and drifting snow, and rail traffic was halted by icy tracks. Things are now beginning to return to normal, with full recovery expected by tomorrow.

Chapter 12: Preparation (pages 111 to 120)

Exercise 12.2
1. There are <u>new</u> allegations of <u>corruption</u> in the upper levels of city government. <u>Documents</u> recently obtained under the Freedom of Information legislation <u>show</u> that as much as <u>one and a half million dollars</u> is <u>unaccounted for</u>.
2. The coach stressed that <u>no one</u> would be <u>benched</u> until tomorrow night's game against the first-place Fangs. He <u>admitted</u>, however, that some <u>drastic action</u> may be needed to get the team <u>back on track</u>.
3. Today is the <u>second anniversary</u> of this city's <u>worst snowstorm</u>. More than <u>half a metre</u> of snow fell in <u>less than six hours</u>, knocking out electricity and shutting down the entire region. The forecast for <u>today</u> is <u>mild</u> by comparison.
4. A local resident is in <u>serious condition</u> at City Hospital after the car she was driving was <u>hit by a slow-moving train</u>. Witnesses say the woman's car <u>stalled on the tracks</u> at the Fifth Street railway crossing, just as the <u>eastbound freight</u> pulled away from the yard.
5. <u>China's</u> government announced today that it would be <u>raising domestic airfares</u> by as much as <u>50</u> percent. The increase comes as a result of that country's move to a <u>freer market economy</u> and the necessity to compete on the world market for <u>fuel</u> and <u>equipment</u>.

Chapter 19: Writing to Sound (pages 170 to 184)

Exercise 19.1
1. (Avoid blind lead-ins.) Tony Jacobs is the site manager for the new building, and he says it is safe. . . .
2. (Identify the speaker.) After a marathon discussion, council finally agreed to refer the budget back to committee. Councillor Barbara Kwan says the problem should have been dealt with now instead of delayed. . . .
3. (Avoid parroting.) There are significant advantages to the new computers, according to ministry spokesman Blair Robbins. . . .
4. The owner of the flooded house, Geraldine Tremont, wants the city to take action. . . .
5. OK

Exercise 19.3
1. a. Voicer
   The bridge over Rock River collapsed sometime during the night after the floodwaters washed away its supports. The unusually high water has been caused by the combination of heavy rain and cold temperatures. Normally, the spring runoff is able to flow down the river, but this year the ice hasn't cleared the river yet and is backing up the rainwater. This bridge is more than 50 years old, and the fast current combined with high water levels just proved to be too much for it. Traffic will be re-routed along Plane Street until the bridge is either repaired or replaced. At the River Road Bridge, this is Maria Fernandez for News Now.

b. Newsreader's copy

Bridge out . . . Apr. 9/96 . . . 8 a.m. . . . MF . . . Cart 16C

Traffic on River Road is being diverted this morning because the bridge is out. News Now's Maria Fernandez says high water is to blame. . . .

> Cart: 16C
> In: The bridge over . . .
> Out: signoff
> Runs: 35 sec

City work crews will have to wait until at least tomorrow to assess the damage and determine whether the bridge can be repaired.

Exercise 19.4

1. Newsreader's copy

New computers . . . Dec. 4/96 . . . 11 p.m. . . . KH . . . Cart 29

The microchip has become a part of just about every profession, and now it is making policing easier. Reporter Kevin Horvath says that police officers in our city are going digital. . . .

> Cart: 29
> In: When an officer . . .
> Out: signoff
> Runs: 55 sec

So . . . add computer literacy to the necessary skills for a police officer in the 21st century.

Exercise 19.5

1. a. Reporter's script

A disappointed team arrived back in town tonight. Favoured to win the championship this year, the Hawks couldn't get past a tough team from Saint Joseph's High School in the semifinals. Leading at the half, they finally lost 86–80. Coach Danny Steinbach was understandably very disappointed when he got off the team bus a few minutes ago. . . .

> Cart: 127
> In: We had it . . .
> Out: . . . maybe next year
> Runs: 09 sec

The team's high scorer in the game was Hank Roiton with 19 points. For News Now sports, this is Gary Parson.

b. Newscaster's script

Team loses . . . Mar. 4/96 . . . 11 p.m. . . . GP . . . Cart 98

The Vincent Massey High School basketball team has been eliminated from the provincial championships. News Now's Gary Parson says the boys are still in shock. . . .

> Cart: 98
> In: A disappointed team . . .
> Out: signoff
> Runs: 45 sec

This is the second year in a row the Hawks have been to the provincial semifinals . . . and the second year in a row they have been beaten by Saint Joseph's.

Index